A GUIDE TO
Wildflowers, Grasses, Aquatic Vegetation,
Trees, Shrubs & Other Flora

D0003232

Plants of the Chesapeake Bay

Lytton John Musselman & David A. Knepper

The Johns Hopkins University Press
BALTIMORE

Contents

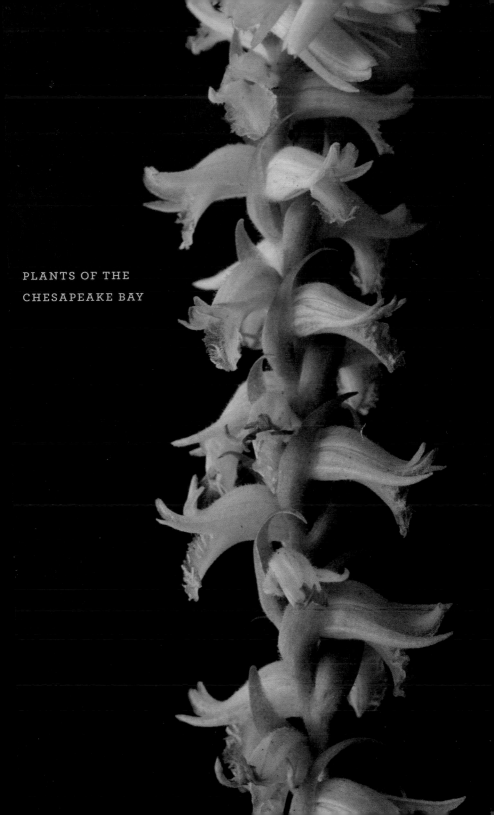

PLANTS OF THE
CHESAPEAKE BAY

(continued)

Acknowledgments

This book builds on the work of many people. Pioneer botanists, among them the very first American plant scientists, were fascinated by Chesapeake Bay plants. While our observations are original, we have confirmed the records of numerous professional botanists, ecologists, and wetland scientists; however, any errors are ours alone.

Jay Bolin, Rebecca Bray, Doug Davis, Nick Flanders, Harold Jones, Tony Matthews, William McAvoy, Bill Micks, Peter Schafran, Don Schwab, Carl Taylor, and Hal Wiggins helped with fieldwork despite river ice, sweltering sun, vermin, mud, and Tearthumb. Robert Lichvar gave unbelievable assistance. David Berg advised on cameras and images. Numerous class and individual field trips at parks and refuges were made possible by the personnel at Chickahominy Riverfront Park, Eastern Shore National Wildlife Refuge, First Landing State Park, Fisherman Island National Wildlife Refuge, Kiptopeke State Park, and Prime Hook National Wildlife Refuge. Our fellow workers at the U.S. Army Corps of Engineers as well as numerous wetland consultants and Old Dominion University students, faculty, and staff have stimulated us with thoughtful questions and provided ecological collegiality.

We are thankful for the generous support of the Mary Payne Hogan endowment that made this project possible. Lastly, as for anyone interested in the Bay, the resources of the Chesapeake Bay Program have been an invaluable resource for us.

This work would not have happened without the support and counsel of Vincent Burke, a poet-editor whose suggestions are manifest in any beneficial parts of the book. We have benefited from the careful editing of Peter Schafran.

We gratefully acknowledge supportive and loving parents and the unflagging love and never-ending encouragement of our wives, Penny Knepper and Libby Musselman.

Introduction

The two authors, between them, have more than seventy-five years of experience in the water, marshes, and shores of Chesapeake Bay. As a result, the plants that grow there have become fast friends and we would like to introduce them to a wider audience. The book is a natural outgrowth of our experiences as a teacher, researcher, wetland biologist, and lovers of the Bay plant communities, and we hope to share our enthusiasm with others through the descriptions, photographs, and lore presented here.

Like any first encounter, it is not possible to know the personalities of these plants without further contact. What we offer are introductions to our plants, not complete resumes: this is not a technical botanical treatment. Such resources are available, and the Chesapeake region is fortunate to have a variety of excellent botanical manuals treating of the entire flora. Among them are the forthcoming *Flora of Virginia,* by J. Christopher Ludwig, Alan S. Weakley, and J. Townsend, and Weakley's online and regularly updated *Flora of the Southern and Mid-Atlantic States.* These in turn build on several regional floras, including *Manual of the Vascular Flora of the Carolinas,* by A. E. Radford, H. A. Ahles, and C. R. Bell; *The Flora of Delaware, an Annotated Checklist,* by W. McAvoy, and K. Bennett; and *Atlas of the Virginia Flora,* by A. M. Harvill Jr. and others. Two other excellent and comprehensive resources are the *Manual of the Vascular Plants of the Northeastern United States and Adjacent Canada* by H. A. Gleason and A. Cronquist and the invaluable, albeit dated, *Gray's Manual of Botany,* 8th edition, by M. L. Fernald. The inquirer who wants to learn more about the plants we include and their relatives should consult one of these. We have used them extensively.

Rather than give technical descriptions, our purpose is to direct the curious to the wonderful panoply of Chesapeake Bay plants with their astounding diversity in habit, color, habitat, phenology, and uses. This might turn out to be like meeting a visitor from a foreign country for the first time and not knowing when you will see the person again. We realize from experience that some of the populations of plants we have been introduced to and were just getting to know are now irretrievably gone, to be replaced by a bulkhead, extirpated by road construction, or engulfed by noxious invaders. If through this book these citizens of the Bay become better known and this results in increased appreciation and protection of these plants, then one of our chief objectives will have been met.

What plants to cover has not proven simple. In general, we treat those in the tidal zone; that is, plants experiencing partial flooding of a portion of the plant diurnally. We do venture out of the water, however, to include representative plants found higher in the marsh, including some dune plants. Coverage is not exhaustive; to have all the plants would require a much larger book.

For ease of field use, we have arranged the plants by the salinity zones in which they are found: super (hyper) saline, maritime, brackish, and fresh. Delineation of these zones is not always clear-cut and there is overlap. But the linking of the plants to salinity enables the user to consider the plants as part of a larger structure. From a practical standpoint, it links plants that will be seen together in one place, as when becoming familiar with a neighborhood and the people who live there.

Within the salinity categories, we arrange plants by their habit—that is, their growth form or appearance—and include trees, shrubs, vines, herbaceous plants, and submerged plants. We envision a reader in, for example, a salt marsh, noting Salt-marsh Cord Grass and wondering what the nearby purple-flowering herbaceous plant is. By looking through the entries for brackish and knowing the plant is herbaceous, Seaside Gerardia will be found.

The idea behind common names is to have pronounceable, familiar names. Some plants have a plethora of common names, like *Nuphar lutea,* called Yellow Water Lily, Spatter Dock, Cow Lily, Water Collard, Water Chinquapin, and Brandy Bottles (from the purported smell of the fruits, resembling brandy). Others, like many species of the large genus *Carex,* have no widely accepted common names. Quill-worts (genus *Isoetes*) are even more depauperate in common names. In general, we use the common names on the U.S. Department of Agriculture Web site. Since that source covers all of North America, some of the common names are not common in the Bay region. So we equivocate and, while in the main following the USDA, on occasion use the names that we believe have the most currency in the Bay region. Alternative common names are listed in the appendix. This, of course, is not an exhaustive treatment. Scientific names, a necessity for further information retrieval, are included.

Synonyms and families are listed in the appendix. There is a formal convention for the use of scientific names, yet many plants have more than one scientific name. These are taxonomic synonyms. Not to worry: any of the scientific names can be used for information retrieval and will take you to the target plant.

Our species descriptions are deliberately short. Descriptions emphasize distinguishing features. We avoid botanical jargon that, if used, would provide twenty terms to describe the hairs on a leaf and a similar number of terms for the arrangement of flowers. Our approach may require more words but it spares the reader the incomprehensibility that would ensue should we lapse into our native botanical tongue. The length of treatments varies simply because there is more to say about some plants than others; some are keystone species or invasive plants requiring more explication. We include what we hope are tantalizing notes about some plants' personalities, arising from our own experience. We say, for example, how plants are used.

The most effective and most accurate way to identify a plant is to have a knowledgeable person tell you about it. We do that through pictures, as well as words. For this work we have amassed thousands of images. From these we chose pictures giving reliable characters for determination. Like many of our readers, we enjoy these plants throughout the year so have tried to include pictures from different seasons. Most are taken during the growing season, when plants are flowering. Except for *Zostera,* images have all been taken especially for this work by the first-named author.

PLANTS OF THE
CHESAPEAKE BAY

Plant Communities of the Chesapeake Bay

Balmy or boisterous, the Chesapeake Bay seeps and surges into the life of all who live on its shores. Daily our weather, our travel patterns, and even our food are influenced by this body of water. It has always been that way for people who lived near it.

Native Americans often lived near the shores of the Bay because of the bounty of seafood and useful plants. Early European settlers drew on the same resource, and the Bay figures prominently in early colonial history. Jamestown, the first permanent English settlement in North America, was established on the banks of the James River, one of the major tributaries to the Bay. Through the years, other settlements followed.

The problem is that now more people than ever live on the Bay. Over the centuries the Bay's bounty has diminished due to a range of stresses, including exploitation of aquatic and terrestrial resources, overdevelopment within the watershed, point and nonpoint source pollution, and habitat loss. For the past 25 years, efforts to clean up the Bay have been spearheaded by a cooperative assemblage of state agencies from the six states in the Bay's watershed (Delaware, Maryland, New York, Pennsylvania, Virginia, and West Virginia), the District of Columbia, federal agencies, recreational and commercial entities dependent on the Bay, environmental groups, and individual members of the public.

The Chesapeake Bay is well known for not only being one of the largest natural estuaries in North America but also for the historically abundant and varied biological resources found within its waters. One of the sources for the Bay's high biodiversity is the range of different habitats present in the Bay and its watershed, and it is plants—the subject of this book—that delineate the majestic rivers, creeks, inlets, and rivulets of this vast estuary, and even parts of its bottom.

Most tidal waters and wetlands in the Chesapeake Bay are limited to Maryland and Virginia, with relatively short stretches of freshwater tidal tributaries extending into Delaware. Although these wetlands present a continuum, it is useful to distinguish among the plant communities. Because each plant's conditions for optimal growth are different, most natural community classification schemes are based on identifying changes in the assemblage of dominant plants along some environmental gradient. The controlling environmental factors for plants growing in tidal areas include, but are not limited to, salinity, water depth, flooding duration, periodic desiccation, wave action, current speed, light availability, suitable substrates, competing vegetation, and herbivory. The Chesapeake Bay is an estuary (which is defined as a semi-enclosed water body where fresh and saltwater intermix), and although there is a general salinity gradient that gradually decreases from the mouth of the Bay up into the headwaters of its main tributaries, five artificial salinity zones can be distinguished (see table 1 and the figure opposite).

Salinity zones in Chesapeake Bay in summer. The most saline parts are in the Bay's southeast, indicated by dark blue. Courtesy of Chesapeake Bay Program

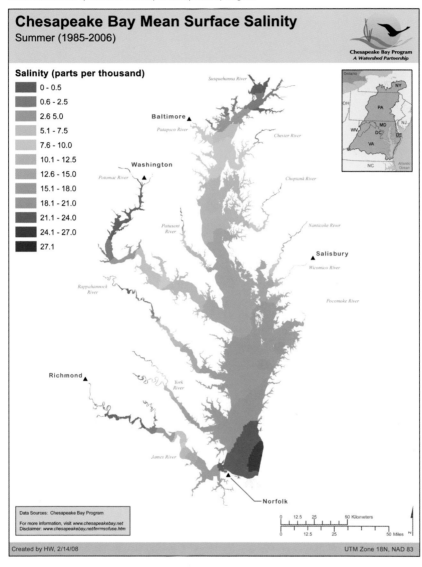

Chesapeake Bay Mean Surface Salinity
Summer (1985-2006)

Chesapeake Bay Program
A Watershed Partnership

Salinity (parts per thousand)

- 0 - 0.5
- 0.6 - 2.5
- 2.6 5.0
- 5.1 - 7.5
- 7.6 - 10.0
- 10.1 - 12.5
- 12.6 - 15.0
- 15.1 - 18.0
- 18.1 - 21.0
- 21.1 - 24.0
- 24.1 - 27.0
- 27.1

Data Sources: Chesapeake Bay Program
For more information, visit *www.chesapeakebay.net*
Disclaimer: *www.chesapeakebay.net/termsofuse.htm*

Created by HW, 2/14/08

UTM Zone 18N, NAD 83

Salinity within the Bay varies regularly in response to the ebb and flood of the tides, prevailing winds, rainfall, freshwater discharges from river tributaries into the Bay, and other factors. Since the rivers are the main sources of freshwater entering the Bay, the extent of saltwater intrusion upriver depends on the elevation

3

and amount of rainfall in the watershed and the resulting storm-water runoff and river discharge. This varies with the size of the different tributaries, but the pattern of decreasing salinity zones extending up the rivers is repeated on all the major tributaries to the Bay. Higher salinities creep northward along the southeastern portion of the Bay because more and larger tributaries empty freshwater into the Bay from the west and north.

TABLE 1 | **Aquatic habitat salinity ranges.**
Adapted from L. M. Cowardin, V. Carter, F. C. Golet, and E. T. LaRoe (1979),
Classification of Wetlands and Deepwater Habitats of the United States

NAME	SALINITY (PARTS PER THOUSAND)
Hyper Saline	greater than 40
Maritime	30 to 40
More Brackish	5 to 30
Less Brackish	0.5 to 5
Freshwater	less than 0.5

We briefly discuss the plant communities found in the Bay in these different salinity zones. Overall, plants exhibit increased habitat fidelity in the more highly stressed high-salinity habitats when compared to the freshwater tidal habitats. Put another way, these saline habitats require more specialization, as reflected in the physiology and morphology of these plants. Additionally, freshwater tidal habitats are more structurally varied (e.g., herbs, shrubs, saplings, trees, and woody vines can be present) than saltier habitats, which are often limited to submergent or herbaceous plants. The plants mentioned in the different salinity-zone descriptions are just the dominant species, and an exhaustive list of plants that occur in these areas is not provided. The communities are circumscribed based on salt expressed as parts per thousand (ppt).

Hyper Saline (salinity greater than 40 ppt)

Salt pans/pannes are localized depressions or areas of poor water circulation just at or above the upper high tide line or the landward edge of salt marshes that are not well flushed during the tidal cycle. Salt pans can be relatively narrow linear features or broad flats covering tens of acres. The rate of evaporation exceeds new water inputs into these areas, resulting in salinity levels that are much higher than that of ocean water. The combination of high salinity and intense solarization creates a harsh habitat that few plants can tolerate. Some representative species found here include glassworts (*Salicornia* spp. and *Sarcocornia perennis*), Sea Lavender (*Limonium carolinianum*), Salt Grass (*Distichlis spicata*), and Seaside Gerardia (*Agalinis maritima*).

Maritime (salinity 30 to 40 ppt)

Only waters at and just inside the mouth of the Bay have salinities equal to that of the Atlantic Ocean. Anyone who has visited the beaches of Cape Charles and Cape Henry at the mouth of the Bay knows that the surf may not always be as strong there as along the unprotected Atlantic Coast, but the salinity, wave action, currents, and winds are still powerful enough to discourage the growth of plants in the shallow waters along the beach.

Although plants are absent from the portion of the sandy beaches subject to daily tidal inundation, vegetation is present above the upper limit of storm tides. Regular salt spray, periodic storms, droughty well-drained sands, nutrient-poor soils, and other factors all limit the kinds of plants that can grow in this maritime zone. Patchy growth of grasses and other herbaceous plants are found on and among the primary dunes. In the secondary dunes, scattered shrubs become more common. Further inland these communities transition into maritime forests. Plants of these maritime communities include Sea Rocket (*Cakile edentula*), Salt-meadow Cord Grass (*Spartina patens*), Japanese Sedge (*Carex kobomugi*), Sea Oats (*Uniola paniculata)* and Bay Berry (*Morella cerifera*), Live Oak (*Quercus virginiana*), and Hercules' Club (*Zanthoxylum clava-herculis*). Many of the plants found here are not naturally found in any other habitat.

Coastal development has eliminated much of the Bay's maritime communities, but good examples persist in semiprotected areas such as national wildlife refuges (e.g., the Eastern Shore of Virginia and Fisherman's Island National Wildlife Refuges), state parks (e.g., First Landing State Park, formerly known as Seashore State Park), and military bases (e.g., the Joint Expeditionary Base Little Creek / Fort Story).

More Brackish (salinity 5 to 30 ppt)

The salinity range "more brackish" encompasses the greatest surface area of the Chesapeake Bay waters extending northward almost to Baltimore. The number of species adapted to live in the more saline brackish waters of the Bay is very limited due to the demands imposed by the physical environment, most importantly the daily tidal fluctuations and high salinity. Structurally the high-salinity brackish plant communities are limited to three main types: salt marshes, shrublands, and underwater beds of submerged aquatic vegetation (SAV).

By definition, marshes are wetlands dominated by herbaceous plants. Salt marshes are comprised of hardy perennials that occur in clearly delimited zones, each of which is dominated by one or two plant species. Lower elevations in the intertidal zone are colonized by extensive, almost pure stands of Salt-marsh Cord Grass (*Spartina alterniflora*). Slightly higher elevations in the marsh can be dominated by dense stands of Black Needle Rush (*Juncus roemarianus*), Salt Grass (*Distichlis spicata*), and/or Salt-meadow Cord Grass (*Spartina patens*). Scattered patches of Salt-marsh Bulrush (*Bolboschoenus robustus*), Sea Oxeye (*Borrichia frutescens*), and Sea Lavender (*Limonium carolinianum*) are common. Along the upper, landward margin of the marsh there is often a shrub community dominated by Groundsel Tree (*Baccharis halimifolia*) and Marsh Elder (*Iva frutescens*). Species diversity is low in this plant community, but overall productivity is high.

Salt marshes are extremely important nursery grounds for crabs and juvenile fish. Additionally, the marshes help protect the shoreline from erosive forces by dampening wave energy and encouraging the deposition of sediments. Since the mid-1970s the acreage of salt-marsh loss due to filling and draining has decreased because of federal and state environmental laws and local ordinances. However, these are dynamic systems and the cumulative effects of shoreline hardening (e.g., bulkheads and riprap revetments) over the years have reduced the flux of sediments to these systems. Some people believe that, deprived of a continual sediment source, the rate of salt-marsh accretion or buildup cannot keep up with the predicted rise in sea level or varied rates of marsh subsidence. For this reason many proponents of Chesapeake Bay restoration advocate the use of "living shorelines" in lieu of hardened structures for shoreline stabilization.

Eel Grass (*Zostera marina*) and Wigeon Grass (*Ruppia maritima*) are the main SAV species found in the saltier brackish Bay waters. Leaf production by these plants is prolific; they not only provide habitat for juvenile fish and crabs but, as the leaves fragment and move with the currents, they also serve as a food source for invertebrates and fish. Beds of SAV also help dampen wave energy, reduce shoreline erosion, and encourage sediment deposition and stabilization. One of the Chesapeake Bay restoration goals is to restore SAV habitat. Historically, an estimated 600,000 acres of SAV were thought to be present before the decline in the Bay's water quality. In 2009, almost 86,000 acres of SAV were mapped for the Bay and its tributaries. Threats to SAV beds include pollution, which degrades water quality, and dredging.

Less Brackish (salinity 0.5 to 5 ppt)

The less-brackish waters in the northern portion of the Bay and middle reaches of the larger tributaries (James River, York River, Potomac River) are still subject to semidiurnal tides, but the lower salinity, among other factors, results in a different suite of dominant plants. The plant diversity is still low, but marshes can be dominated by relatively pure stands of Big Cord Grass (*Spartina cynosuroides*), Narrowleaf Cattail (*Typha angustifolia*), Common Reed (*Phragmites australis*), Wild Rice (*Zizania aquatica*), and Southern Wild Rice (*Zizaniopsis miliacea*). Common shrubs in these systems include Bay Berry, Marsh Elder, and Swamp Rose (*Rosa palustris*).

The dominant SAV species are still Eel Grass and Wigeon Grass.

Threats to these systems are similar to those of the more saline brackish communities. For ease in using the book, we combine the two brackish communities.

Freshwater (salinity less than 0.5 ppt)

Freshwater tidal communities are subject to two tidal cycles per day, but have average salinities of less than 0.5 ppt. In the Chesapeake Bay, these systems are geographically limited to the extreme north, near the mouth of the Susquehanna River, and the upper reaches of the other larger tributaries. Of all the Bay tidal wetlands, freshwater tidal communities support the greatest number of plant species. Zonation is less distinct and driven more by competition with other plant species than by stressful environmental conditions. In terms of structure (i.e., the number of different strata), the tidal freshwater communities are also more diverse than the more saline tidal areas. In addition to marshes and SAV beds, freshwater tidal systems have zones of floating aquatics and extensive swamp shrublands and forests. The majority of plants found in freshwater tidal waters are not limited to areas influenced by tides but can also be found in a range of inland, nontidal wetlands. Unlike other tidal systems in the Bay, the character of freshwater tidal communities changes drastically seasonally. The lush, densely vegetated marshes and beds of floating-leaved and submerged aquatics in the summer and spring transform into bare mudflats during the fall and winter, when the aboveground biomass breaks down and is exported to downstream waters.

SAVs and floating-leaved aquatics are found in the portions of the waterway that are too deep for emergent herbs to become established. Representative species include Common Hornwort (*Ceratophyllum demersum*), the egregious invasive Hydrilla (*Hydrilla verticillata*), Southern Water Nymph (*Najas guadalupensis*), and Yellow Pond Lily (*Nuphar lutea*).

The lower intertidal zone is characterized by diminutive plants with a grass-like growth habit, and they are often overlooked. These include Pipewort (*Eriocaulon parkeri*), Waterwort (*Elatine americana*), and quillworts (*Isoetes* spp.). The upper part of the intertidal zone is characterized by a broad and diverse assemblage of species, such as Wild Rice, Southern Wild Rice, Pickerel Weed (*Pontederia cordata*), Arrow Arum (*Peltandra virginica*), cattails (*Typha* spp.), smartweeds (*Persicaria* spp.—formerly in the genus *Polygonum*), Beggar's Ticks (*Bidens* spp.), and Jewelweed (*Impatiens capensis*).

Buttonbush (*Cephalanthus occidentalis*), Brookside Alder (*Alnus serrulata*), Bay Berry (*Morella cerifera*), and Swamp Rose (*Rosa palustris*) are some of the dominant shrubs found in the higher elevations of the marsh. Seaside Alder (*Alnus maritima*) is locally abundant in some freshwater tidal marshes of Delaware and Maryland.

Freshwater tidal swamps are characterized by Bald Cypress (*Taxodium distichum*), Green Ash (*Fraxinus pennsylvanica*), Pumpkin Ash (*Fraxinus profunda*), Black Gum (*Nyssa biflora*), Red Maple (*Acer rubrum*), Sweet Gum (*Liquidambar styraciflua*), American Holly (*Ilex opaca*), Sweetbay Magnolia (*Magnolia virginiana*), and Ironwood (*Carpinus caroliniana*). Understory species include Spicebush (*Lindera benzoin*), Winterberry (*Ilex verticillata*), Tall Pawpaw (*Asimina triloba*), Fetterbush (*Leucothoe racemosa*), Arrow Arum (*Peltandra virginica*), Halberd-leaved Tearthumb

(*Persicaria arifolium*), Lizard Tail (*Saururus cernuus*), and Common Greenbrier (*Smilax rotundifolia*).

Threats to freshwater tidal systems include impoundment from construction of dams, municipal water withdrawals, and saltwater intrusion from sea-level rise. Invasive species such as Common Reed (*Phragmites australis*) and cattails (*Typha* spp.) can also be problematic because they quickly colonize disturbed sites. Being situated at the confluence of nontidal and tidal environments, freshwater tidal communities are more susceptible to changes in water quality resulting from agriculture and development in the contributing watershed.

PLANTS OF THE
CHESAPEAKE BAY

PLANTS OF

Hyper Saline Habitats

(From left to right)
Samphire, *Salicornia virginica*, in its crimson autumnal glory. These plants are about 1.5 ft. tall.

The three species of Bay glassworts in late summer. Samphire, Dwarf Glasswort with its fat stems, and Perennial Glasswort, with long, thin, creeping stems.

Dwarf Glasswort, *Salicornia bigelovii*, characterized by very thick stems and diminutive stature; about 10 in. tall.

Glassworts, *Salicornia* species

Glassworts draw attention because they look so unplant-like. There are no typical leaves. Instead, the plant body consists of a series of succulent jointed segments, which can turn a brilliant scarlet color in the late autumn. Flowers are small and project out of the fleshy stem.

DISTINGUISHING FEATURES: Without typical leaves, a population of glassworts looks like pop beads stacked together. Flowers are very small and rudimentary, peeping out from the thick, fleshy stems. Seeds are tiny and fuzzy, perhaps an adaption to water dispersal. In addition to their peculiar anatomy, glassworts are also highly specialized for their habitat. They are halophytes—plants able to thrive in soils of extreme salinity. For this reason they are found in the saltiest regions of the Bay.

But what is glassy about these plants? The name glasswort comes from the ancient practice of burning these and related species for soda ash, necessary in certain types of glass manufacture. The formal classification of this group is in a state of flux, so this treatment must be considered provisional.

HABITAT: These are extreme halophytes. Some are able to germinate in a 45% salt solution so they often form dense stands in marshes where saltwater overflows and then evaporates. There are three species in the Bay, frequently found growing together.

1. Perennial Glasswort, *Sarcocornia perennis*, confusingly also known as *Salicornia virginica* (see description below). Common in saline mudflats, this perennial sends out shoots that root in the mud. Over time the plant develops a mound-like structure as it grows, accumulating detritus and stabilizing the substrate. This species has the narrowest stem of any of our glassworts.
2. Samphire, *Salicornia depressa*, frequently known as *Salicornia europaea*, is an annual. It can be recognized by having the segments of the stem noticeably longer than wide.
3. Dwarf Glasswort, *Salicornia bigelovii*. As this is the most obese of the glassworts, with segments about as wide as long, the common name may seem misleading. It refers to the stature, not the girth of the plant.

WILDLIFE/ECOLOGICAL VALUE: Little known.

HUMAN USES: In addition to use in glass manufacture that requires soda ash, glassworts are edible and considered a delicacy in some European countries.

Flowers of Sea Lavender vary from light blue to purple, with occasional plants having white flowers. The flowers are visited by bees and butterflies.

(*Opposite*)
Masses of flowers from a much-branched Sea Lavender. They are small and widely spaced, a mass of these plants producing a kind of blue mist.

Sea Lavender, *Limonium carolinianum*

Sea Lavender is a descriptive name for this common component of salt marshes throughout the Bay because of its lavender-colored flowers. It belongs to a family that contains many species adapted to habitats with high salinity.

DISTINGUISHING FEATURES: The prominent basal leaves of this deep-rooted perennial and the much-branched, almost wispy, wiry stems with blue (rarely white) flowers make this plant easy to recognize. Leaves are entire (with smooth, untoothed margins) up to 5 in. long, seldom more than 2 in. wide, with a slightly leathery texture. The flowers are small, up to 0.6 in. long. They appear in the summer. Fruits are small and nut-like.

HABITAT: A true halophyte, Sea Lavender grows with other obligate halophytes like glassworts, Sea Oxeye, and Salt Grass.

CONFUSED WITH: Easily recognized when flowering. The basal rosettes, when sterile, can resemble Seaside Aster, but are generally larger. Leaves of Seaside Goldenrod are also similar, but much larger than Sea Lavender.

WILDLIFE/ECOLOGICAL VALUE: None recorded.

HUMAN USES: The flowering branches are sometimes collected and dried for floral arrangements; they are similar to the Statice of the florist, *Limonium sinuatum*. At least one other species, *Limonium latifolium*. is used as a planting near seawater due to its tolerance of salt.

Seaside Gerardia is often densely branched. In the photo opposite, some developing fruits can be seen at the top of the plant.

Seaside Gerardia, *Agalinis maritima*

This is a modest, charming fall-flowering annual. Like other members of the genus, it obtains water and nutrients by forming underground attachments to the roots of host plants. Its devious botanical behavior is not obvious. Various plants serve as hosts. We have found Salt Grass to be one of the most frequent.

DISTINGUISHING FEATURES: Rarely more than 10 in. tall, Seaside Gerardia is usually much branched and has opposite, fleshy leaves with a sandpaper-like feel and conspicuous purple flowers. The flowers last for only one day so it is best to visit the plants on a sunny morning. By late afternoon, the flowers, often battered by frequent insect visits, fall to the ground.

HABITAT: Restricted to salt marshes, this is a true halophyte.

WILDLIFE/ECOLOGICAL VALUE: None known.

HUMAN USES: None known.

A flowering specimen of Southern Sea Blite in midsummer.

Southern Sea Blite, *Suaeda linearis*

Other species of this genus are found in saline habitats around the world. The Latin name is derived from Arabic in reference to similar plants in salty deserts of the Middle East.

DISTINGUISHING FEATURES: The fleshy leaves of this annual plant are round in cross section. Flowers are small, green, and unremarkable.

HABITAT: Southern Sea Blite has a restricted distribution in the Bay because of its preference for high salinity.

CONFUSED WITH: It is not easily confused with anything because of the distinctive leaves.

WILDLIFE/ECOLOGICAL VALUE: None recorded.

HUMAN USES: The entire plant, including the seeds, is edible and has a pleasant salty taste. Species of *Suaeda*, like glassworts, were harvested and burned to obtain the sodium carbonate (soda ash) and other compounds used in the manufacture of glass.

PLANTS OF

Maritime Habitats

Eel Grass, *Zostera marina*

It is not an exaggeration to say that Eel Grass is one of the most important submersed plants in the Bay. The once vast beds have been dramatically reduced to a fraction of their original extent. Most beach walkers have seen the strands of strap-like dark-green leaves on the wrack line.

DISTINGUISHING FEATURES: Eel Grass is part of a guild of plants known as sea grasses. These remarkable plants are the only group of flowering plants growing submersed in the ocean. They are rooted perennials with nitrogen-fixing organisms in their roots. Leaves are strap-shaped, up to 30 in. long, with parallel margins and a rounded tip. This is the part of the plant that most people are familiar with, seeing the blackish-green leaves strewn on Bay beaches. Flowers are produced in the spring and are unisexual. Tiny in size, they are engineered for their marine habitat. Unlike most plants, pollen is released in long, sticky strings. As the strings move through the water they entangle on to the feathery, receptive female flowers. Seeds are tiny and also water dispersed.

HABITAT: Named because of its grass-like appearance, Eel Grass once carpeted much of the bottom of Chesapeake Bay in brackish to saline water, providing provender and shelter for a diversity of organisms. A blight of Eel Grass appeared in the Bay in the 1930s, destroying massive numbers of plants. That devastation, followed by increased shoreline destruction and pollution, has reduced populations. An active replanting program is now under way.

CONFUSED WITH: There are no other submersed plants in the marine portions of the Bay that have dark-green, strap-like leaves (*zostera* means strap) with rounded tips.

WILDLIFE/ECOLOGICAL VALUE: It is hard to overestimate the role of this keystone species in the ecology of the Bay. Many marine organisms depend on the plants for shelter and food.

HUMAN USES: It was once harvested from the shoreline or raked at low tide and used as a green manure. In Scandinavia, Eel Grass was used to stuff mattresses, a use that is credible for anyone who has handled the resilient dried leaves.

Beach Grass in deep coastal sand (*opposite*). The flowering stalks are narrow and erect. Like all grasses, the flowers are small and inconspicuous (*right*).

Beach Grass, *Ammophila breviligulata*

Few plants can thrive in the deep, shifting sands of dunes, but this is the favorite habitat of Beach Grass. The long, tough, underground stems extend through the sand, producing roots and shoots that stabilize the dune by trapping and holding sand.

DISTINGUISHING FEATURES: This is a tough, resilient plant, the stormtrooper of the plant world, and it can occupy the dune closest to the water, stabilize the dune, and as a result make it suitable for other plants. The leaves are about 3.3 ft. long and 2 in. wide, with the narrow flowering and fruiting stalk rising to about 4 ft. Flowers appear in midsummer. As with all true grasses, the flowers are unremarkable. In early fall, numerous hard grains are produced.

HABITAT: Dunes around the Bay. Widely distributed in eastern North America.

CONFUSED WITH: Two other grasses regularly grow with Beach Grass. The best known is Sea Oats (*Uniola paniculata*), which has large, flattened, drooping grains. Beach Panic Grass (*Panicum amarum*) also grows with Beach Grass, but further shoreward. It has a grey-green color, with narrow leaves.

WILDLIFE/ECOLOGICAL VALUE: Provides microhabitats for small animals and other plants.

HUMAN USES: The leaves are used for baskets and thatch; also used in dune stabilization.

25

Beach Panic Grass in flower in midsummer.
(*Opposite*) The left photo shows fruits (grains).
Not all Beach Panic Grass has the grey, waxy covering
shown in the right photo.

Beach Panic Grass, *Panicum amarum*

One of the most common grasses on dunes, Beach Panic Grass has a distinctive grey hue that distinguishes it from its cohorts. The common name comes from the scientific name; *panicum* is the Latin word for a kind of millet.

DISTINGUISHING FEATURES: This inhabitant of Bay fore dunes arises from a dense, woody clump. Leaves are tough and evergreen, like its congener Sea Oats, and can survive blowing sand and saltwater. The narrow flowering stalks are about 6.5 ft. tall and narrow, bearing masses of small flowers and eventually grains. A feature of this plant is an often bluish tint, a characteristic that is variable within any population.

HABITAT: One of the most common plants in fore dunes in the Bay.

CONFUSED WITH: *Panicum amarulum* is a closely related and similar-appearing species. The two species are distinguished by technical features of the flowers and rhizomes and are sometimes treated as one, variable species.

WILDLIFE/ECOLOGICAL VALUE: Grazed by cattle. Often planted for dune restoration.

HUMAN USES: Some strains of Beach Panic Grass have been selected for garden planting. The bluish color is attractive.

Sandbur can spread by roots that develop from the stems buried in the sand (*opposite*).

Flowers and fruits are contained in the burs that break from the plant when ripe.

Sandbur, *Cenchrus longispinus*

Bane of barefoot beachcombers, this highly specialized grass distributes its seeds in an armored case that can be carried by animals, including humans.

DISTINGUISHING FEATURES: Sandbur, also known as Sandspur, is seldom more than 1.6 ft. tall. Flowers are produced midsummer. Burs are mature in late summer and early fall.

HABITAT: A native grass, Sandbur favors sandy soils. Dunes and beaches are an ideal habitat for it.

CONFUSED WITH: Easily confused with other grasses when not in fruit.

WILDLIFE/ECOLOGICAL VALUE: A good sand binder. The seeds (grains) are eaten by small mammals.

HUMAN USES: Victims of this plant find it amazing that Sandbur is sometimes grown for its fodder value. Explanation: the grass is cut before the burs develop.

Sea Oats grow closer to the Bay waters than most salinity tolerant grasses (*opposite*).

Fruits of Sea Oats are retained into winter.

Sea Oats, *Uniola paniculata*

The best-known and most easily recognized of any of the many grasses native to the Bay, Sea Oats is restricted to dunes. It is an important soil binder.

DISTINGUISHING FEATURES: Arising from strong, resilient, underground stems, this perennial grass has long, tough leaves that persist through the winter and can survive the overwash of seawater. Flowers and fruits are produced on tall, separate stalks that rise to about 6 ft. The flat clusters of grains are diagnostic for this species. The few seeds produced are often difficult to germinate.

HABITAT: Sea Oats grows in deep sand and can tolerate salinity. The Bay region is the northern limit of this attractive grass.

WILDLIFE/ECOLOGICAL VALUE: Frequently planted for dune stabilization from cuttings of the rootstock due to the poor germination of the seeds.

HUMAN USES: The grains are edible.

Beach Spurge is one of the first plants encountered on a dune when walking up from the Bay waters. Flowers and developing fruits can be seen in the photo at right.

Beach Spurge, *Chamaesyce polygonifolia*

Beach Spurge is one of a coterie of beach plants that can live on bare sand. Also known as *Euphorbia polygonifolia*.

DISTINGUISHING FEATURES: A small, annual prostrate from a deep taproot, Beach Spurge is easily overlooked in favor of its more showy neighbors like Sea Oats. It has a milky latex when broken. The flowers, which are the size of a pin head, are complex.

HABITAT: Beach Spurge, a true native of the Bay, grows only on the lower reaches of beach dunes, not inland.

CONFUSED WITH: Nothing; however, many species in this genus are found in a diversity of habitats throughout the region. This is the only one growing on beaches.

WILDLIFE/ECOLOGICAL VALUE: By stabilizing even a bit of the sand, this small plant creates habitat for the establishment of other plants.

HUMAN USES: Beach Spurge is likely poisonous, though its small demeanor and clinging sand scarcely make it appealing.

The creeping stems of Beach Vitex rapidly colonize bare sand and crowd out native and desirable plants. Flowers are attractive, one of the reasons it was first introduced to the Atlantic Coast.

Beach Vitex, *Vitex rotundifolia*

One of the common names given to this recent, aggressive invader of Bay dunes and beaches is Beach Kudzu, the well-known vine that blankets acres of southern forests. Beach Vitex has the potential of rapidly growing over large sections of beach. This dangerous plant is being monitored at several places in the Carolinas.

DISTINGUISHING FEATURES: Beach Vitex is a woody plant, a creeping shrub that sends out runners that root and establish the plants. Leaves are round, 2 in. long. Flowers are an attractive blue and produce fruits with numerous seeds. The plant can spread by seed or by extension of runners. In high tides and storms, runners can break off and spread to new areas.

HABITAT: A Korean native, Beach Vitex was first introduced to South Carolina in the 1960s and it has since rapidly spread along the coast of North Carolina into the beaches of the southern Bay, where an eradication program is in place.

WILDLIFE/ECOLOGICAL VALUE: Aggressive invader that displaces native plants.

HUMAN USES: Other members of the genus are valued timber trees in the tropics.

A large Marsh Fleabane at the edge of a salt flat.

Marsh Fleabane, *Pluchea odorata*

The specific epithet of the scientific name says a lot about this plant. The distinctive odor is purported to repel insects. The purple flowers add a distinct color to salt-marsh vegetation.

DISTINGUISHING FEATURES: The most prominent feature of this annual plant is the strong odor (*fragrance* would be too delicate a description for it). It has overtones of camphor. The constituents of the plant that provide the odor are purported to control fleas; hence, the common name. Stems are up to 4 ft. Leaves are alternate, toothed, and about 5 in. long. Heads of attractive purple flowers are produced in the summer and fall. The fruits, produced in autumn, are dispersed by wind; they resemble the fruits of Dandelion. A true halophyte, Marsh Fleabane grows in some of the most saline parts of the Bay.

CONFUSED WITH: No other plant in this habitat has flowers of this purple color and with the distinctive odor.

WILDLIFE/ECOLOGICAL VALUE: None recorded.

HUMAN USES: Used to repel insects. Many humans, too, find the smell to be repulsive.

Sea Rocket in flower (*opposite*). Each seed is contained in a buoyant saltwater-proof casing that allows for water transport (*below*).

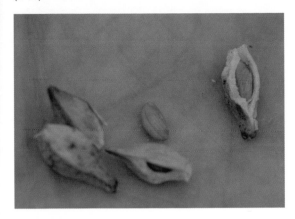

Sea Rocket, *Cakile edentula*

This rocket has nothing to do with NASA. Rocket is likely a corruption of roquette, one of the names of *Eruca sativa*, also known as Arugula, in reference to a similarity in taste of the two plants.

DISTINGUISHING FEATURES: Sea Rocket can have a single stem or many stems arising from the base. Plants are seldom more than 3.5 ft. tall. Leaves are toothed, alternate, and fleshy. Flowers are small, white to purplish, with four petals arranged like a cross.

HABITAT: A dune or beach plant, Sea Rocket grows closer to the Bay waters than almost any other plant. It is found along both the Atlantic and Pacific coasts of North America as well as in similar habitats of the Great Lakes. In the spring, hundreds of new plants are found just above the high tide mark; only a few of these survive into the summer.

CONFUSED WITH: No other plant occupies this habitat.

WILDLIFE/ECOLOGICAL VALUE: None recorded.

HUMAN USES: The leaves have a pleasant mustard taste. There are reports of Native Americans harvesting the roots for food.

Seaside Goldenrod, *Solidago sempervirens*

There are many goldenrods in the Middle Atlantic States, but only one in saline soils, the Seaside Goldenrod. This attractive plant flowers about the same time and often in the same location as Groundsel Tree.

DISTINGUISHING FEATURES: A large perennial up to 5 ft. tall, Seaside Goldenrod flowers in the late summer to early fall. It has attractive masses of lemon-yellow flowers. The one-seeded fruits appear in late autumn and are carried by the wind, being equipped with the botanical equivalent of silky parachutes. Unlike most other goldenrods, this species is evergreen, as the species epithet *sempervirens* indicates.

HABITAT: Frequent in salt marshes, but also on dunes and in disturbed, brackish areas.

CONFUSED WITH: The young leaves resemble those of Sea Lavender.

WILDLIFE/ECOLOGICAL VALUE: Planted for dune restoration.

HUMAN USES: In addition to restoration uses, occasionally planted in gardens for its attractive color and salt tolerance.

TREES AND SHRUBS

Because Bay Berry has unisexual plants, not all shrubs have the characteristic wax-covered fruits.

An alternate name for this fragrant shrub is Wax Myrtle. Like many of the common names in the eastern United States, the name Wax Myrtle is based on the fancy that this shrub resembles a Bible plant, in this case myrtle (*Myrtus communis*), as both have evergreen leaves and a pleasant fragrance. They are unrelated. Wax Myrtle is sometimes put in the genus *Myrica*.

DISTINGUISHING FEATURES: One of the most striking features of this shrub is the vividness of its green color. This is due to the presence of a microorganism living in the roots that has the remarkable ability to convert atmospheric nitrogen into a form the plant can use, a built-in fertilizer source. Bay Berry often grows in soils with very low nutrients, such as sand dunes, but this much-branched shrub's ability to use atmospheric nitrogen enables it to grow rapidly and maintain its characteristic green color when neighboring plants look anemic. The leaves are borne in an alternate manner and are irregularly toothed. The sexes are on separate shrubs. The inconspicuous flowers are borne in the spring and dispersed by wind, which transfers pollen. The fruits are encrusted with wax, hence the species name, *cerifera* (waxy). This wax was used by settlers for candles with a pleasant aroma. This custom lives on in factory-produced candles known as Bay Berry candles.

Fruits of Northern Wax Myrtle (*left*) and Bay Berry (*right*).

Bay Berry, *Morella cerifera*

CONFUSED WITH: Northern Wax Myrtle (*Morella pensylvanica*). This species is not as widely distributed as Bay Berry and is much less common in the Bay region. It is more abundant further north. Northern Wax Myrtle has larger fruits than Bay Berry, stouter twigs, and is not evergreen.

WILDLIFE/ECOLOGICAL VALUE: Because it houses microorganisms that can convert atmospheric nitrogen into a form that plants can use, Bay Berry is of great importance in dune systems low in nitrogen. The fallen leaves add nutrients to the sterile sand.

HUMAN USES: Bay Berry has a variety of uses in addition to being a source of wax. The fruits are edible (though wax covered), and the leaves have been used as an analgesic.

The Hackberry's flowers (*right*) yield the brown fruits in the fall (*below*). Unlike many trees, individual Hackberry trees usually produce fruit consistently each year.

Hackberry, *Celtis laevigata*

Hackberry grows close to edge of a salt marsh. When they are older, these trees give the impression of being slightly plump, with rounded branches and a stocky trunk. The warty grey bark is unlike any other tree in this habitat.

DISTINGUISHING FEATURES: Hackberry can become a tall tree, up to 70 ft., with large, spreading lateral branches. It has a tolerance for salinity. The leaves, about 5 in. long, are arranged in an alternate manner and have an asymmetrical base. Flowers are green, appear in the early spring just as the leaves are developing, and produce mahogany-colored, one-seeded fruits. Surrounding the large seed is a papery layer of very sweet tissue, providing another common name for this tree, Sugarberry.

HABITAT: Hackberry is a characteristic tree along the margins of salt marshes in the Bay. It is widespread across much of the United States.

CONFUSED WITH: The bark of Hackberry is distinct from any other tree in the Bay region.

WILDLIFE/ECOLOGICAL VALUE: The fruits are relished by birds.

HUMAN USES: Fruits are edible. Widely planted in urban areas for its tolerance of salinity and compacted soils.

(*Opposite*) Warty, grey bark is characteristic of the trunk of Hackberry.

A large Hercules' Club in fruit

The leaf of Hercules' Club showing the abundant oil glands that appear as clear dots. At the base of each pair of leaflets are two spines (*left*). The small fruits resemble oranges until they open to expose the black seeds.

Hercules' Club, *Zanthoxylum clava-herculis*

Hercules' Club is one of our most distinctive trees of the Bay. It reaches its northern limit on the Delmarva Peninsula and extends down the Coastal Plain to Florida. Sometimes spelled *Xanthoxylum*.

DISTINGUISHING FEATURES: Hercules' Club is a small tree, up to 20 ft., with an unbranched trunk. Both stem and leaves are armored. Sharp spines are found at the base of each of the 5 to 7 divisions of the leaf. Large, prominent, thorn-like structures arm the trunk. Volatile oils are found throughout the plant, indicating its relation to citrus species and rue.

Plants are unisexual; that is, they are either male or female. The small, insect-pollinated flowers are borne in the early spring, and by early autumn the round, fleshy fruits are maturing. Like the rind of an orange, the fruit contains abundant oil cells. This cracks open to release the one or two seeds, which hang from the fruit, perhaps to increase visibility to birds.

HABITAT: Hercules' Club is found at the very highest part of the beach, where overflow is infrequent.

WILDLIFE/ECOLOGICAL VALUE: The flowers are visited by a diversity of insects, among them butterflies. Birds eat the seeds.

HUMAN USES: There are reports of the dried leaves being used for tea, but this is best avoided due to the potentially harmful chemicals found in the plant. However, in Nepal dried fruits of a species of *Zanthoxylum* are used as a spice. Any use of the plant requires caution.

A characteristic winter scene along Bay dunes. Dune Bluegrass (*Schizachyrium littorale*, sometimes known as *Andropogon virginicus*) in its hibernal coloration, with a slanted tree line of Live Oaks in the background, sculptured by salt and sand blowing from the Bay.

Live Oak, *Quercus virginiana*

Highly tolerant of salinity and hurricanes, these beautiful, evergreen trees are able to survive next to Bay inlets and behind dune systems.

DISTINGUISHING FEATURES: A large, spreading tree up to 80 ft. tall, with massive branches and evergreen leaves, this tree is a memorable feature of the Bay landscape in its southern regions. As with all oaks, the leaves, about 3 in. long, are arranged alternately. In this species, leaves are evergreen, but this does not mean that the tree does not lose its leaves. In the spring, the Live Oak practices what is known as leaf replacement, newly formed leaves replacing older leaves. As the new leaves mature, the older ones are dropped. Flowers are small and inconspicuous, yielding acorns in the fall. The acorns are tasty and were an important food for Native Americans.

HABITAT: One of our most salt-tolerant trees, Live Oak can compete in areas with saltwater flooding. For this reason it is the only oak found close to beaches and along inlets. It is not, however, restricted to marine habitats and is found over a wide range and diversity of habitats in the southern states. In marine habitats, the crowns are pruned back by salt spray and blowing sand, giving the maritime forest a slanted appearance.

CONFUSED WITH: Blue Jack Oak (*Quercus incana*), which reaches its northern limit at the southern edge of the Bay. Blue Jack Oak is also salt tolerant, although much less so than Live Oak. Unlike Live Oak with which it grows, Blue Jack Oak is

A magisterial Live Oak on the edge of the Bay showing the massive side branches and characteristic bark (*opposite*). The thick, evergreen leaves with developing acorns are shown in the photo below.

Live Oak (continued)

deciduous and has thinner leaves. Blue Jack Oak seldom reaches the size of Live Oak. Its acorns have flat cup scales, not the thickened cup scales of Live Oak. Black Jack Oak nuts are also smaller than those of Live Oak.

WILDLIFE/ECOLOGICAL VALUE: The acorns are a valuable food source for wild-life.

HUMAN USES: The timber of Live Oak was valued in building wooden ships, especially the large, curved side branches that could be used for bows and other parts of the ship that needed strong, durable beams. Live Oak acorns are tasty and were widely used by indigenous peoples for food.

PLANTS OF

Brackish Habitats

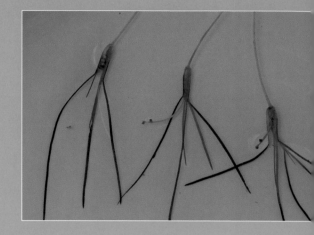

Stages of flowering in Wigeon Grass. In the first plant shown, the mature flowers are within the sheathing leaf base; the two plants at right are developing fruit on the elongate stalks.

Wigeon Grass, *Ruppia maritima*

The common name of this submersed plant is taken from the waterfowl known as wigeon, or widgeon, which, like many other waterfowl, use Wigeon Grass for food. It is not a true grass but has leaves that are grass-like.

DISTINGUISHING FEATURES: A rooted submergent with long flexuous stems that bear usually opposite, linear leaves 1 to 3 in. long. Flowers are inconspicuous and adapted to water pollination. The male parts rise to the water surface, the pollen is released in raft-like masses. The rafts come in contact with the female parts. After fertilization, the fruits are pulled beneath the surface on coiled stems. As winter approaches, Wigeon Grass, like several other hydrophytes, forms specialized buds for overwintering. These break off and allow the plant to spread.

HABITAT: Wigeon Grass is a plant of saline and brackish waters, often forming large, tangled masses by the end of the growing season.

CONFUSED WITH: Easily confused with Sago Pondweed (*Potamogeton pectinatus*). The two often grow together. Wigeon Grass can be readily distinguished by the fruits on coiled stems.

WILDLIFE/ECOLOGICAL VALUE: Wildlife managers often plant Wigeon Grass as food for waterfowl. It also stabilizes the substrate in aquatic systems.

HUMAN USES: None recorded.

A brackish marsh dominated by Three-square Bulrush in late summer.

Bulrushes, species of *Bolboschoenus* & *Schoenoplectus*

Bulrush, the common name, like many original American names of plants, came from the King James Version of the Bible—from the story of Moses being hidden in the bulrushes of the Nile (Exodus 2:3). These most likely were not true bulrushes, but the name has stuck. Strong but modest plants, bulrushes occupy extensive areas of Bay marshes; they are keystone species in aquatic and marine systems. We here consider three of the most common bulrushes in the Chesapeake: Three-square Bulrush (*Schoenoplectus americanus*), Soft-stem Bulrush (*Schoenoplectus tabernaemontani*), and Salt-marsh Bulrush (*Bolboschoenus robustus*).

DISTINGUISHING FEATURES: All bulrushes are grass-like plants from a hearty rootstock. Typical leaves are lacking, and in most the plant consists of a stem with small, inconspicuous flowers that yield hard, shiny, grain-like fruits.

1. Three-square Bulrush. This is the easiest bulrush to identify in the brackish and freshwater marshes of the Bay because it has a sharply three-angled stem. The flower clusters are not on extended stems and the modified leaf at the base of the flowers is erect, appearing as an extension of the stem.
2. Soft-stem Bulrush. Can be up to 6.6 ft. tall. Near the top of the stem the flowers are borne on a cluster of short branches. Like Three-square Bulrush, this species has a modified leaf at the base of the flowers, looking like a simple continuation of the stem.
3. Salt-marsh Bulrush. This species thrives in soils of higher salinity. It has the largest flower clusters and largest grains of any of our bulrushes.

A dense stand of Soft-stem Bulrush at the edge of a brackish marsh. The photo at right shows flowers of this species.

Bulrushes (continued)

CONFUSED WITH: Two other bulrush species are found in the Bay, but infrequently. These are Torrey's Bulrush (*Schoenoplectus torreyi*) and River Bulrush (*Bolboschoenus fluviatilis*). The former resembles Three-square Bulrush, but has fruits triangular in cross section. The latter have numerous leaf-like structures at the base of the flowering branch.

WILDLIFE/ECOLOGICAL VALUE: Bulrushes are keystone species in the extensive brackish and freshwater marshes of the Bay. Frequently they are the dominant plants. In addition to habitat for birds and other animals, bulrushes produce copious amounts of fruit, which is eaten by animals. Their extensive root systems help stabilize marshes.

HUMAN USES: Bay bulrush species have been used for weaving mats and chair bottoms, as well as for food. The potato-like storage organs contain large amounts of starch. All of these bulrushes have edible fruits, which can be ground into flour to make a coarse bread.

(*Clockwise from top left*) Salt-marsh Bulrush in fruit. Fruits of Salt-marsh Bulrush, shown with the smaller fruits from Three-square Bulrush. Tubers, the largest the size of a small potato, from Soft-stem Rush; these develop as swellings in a tough underground (or underwater) stem. Salt-marsh Bulrush, Soft-stem Bulrush, and Three-square Bulrush; in cross-section, the only one of the three not to have a round stem is Three-square Bulrush.

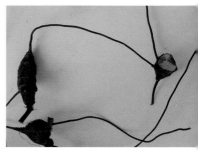

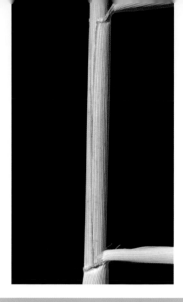

A dense monoculture of Common Reed at the upper margin of a salt marsh. Note the tall leafy stems and dark-brown flowering heads. The stem (*right*) is likely from the native subspecies, but more than one characteristic is essential to verify subspecies. Even in this winter image, leaf sheaths are intact.

Common Reed, *Phragmites australis*

Common Reed is probably the most infamous invasive plant species in Bay wetlands. An aggressive invader of natural marshes and disturbed wetland areas, it often forms large, monospecific stands.

Comprehensive efforts to quantify the extent and rate of Common Reed expansion in the Bay are just starting (e.g., Virginia Division of Natural Heritage's Web-based Virginia Phragmites Mapping Application). Substantial resources have been expended for its control, and several Bay states offer a Common Reed control cost-share program to residents.

For years, botanists postulated that all Common Reed in North America originated from an introduction along the eastern seaboard more than 200 years ago, but paleobotanists have identified Common Reed rhizome fragments in the Coastal Plain dating back a few thousand years, indicating it is a part of the native flora. Recent genetic research identified three subspecies of Common Reed. In the eastern United States, the native subspecies has been commonly supplanted by introduced subspecies, but one of the strongholds for the native *Phragmites australis* is along the major tributaries to Chesapeake Bay, on the eastern shore of Maryland.

The identification of subspecies can be tricky; the treatment below describes only the general characteristics of Common Reed overall.

DISTINGUISHING FEATURES: A tall, leafy-stemmed perennial grass, 6 to 15 ft. tall, that forms dense stands, often excluding native plants. It has a large, terminal-flowering head (approximately 10 in. tall by 6 in. wide) that is brown when the seeds are mature.

Common Reed spreads vegetatively by an extensive network of rhizomes, or underground stems. It can colonize new, distant sites by seeds that are dispersed by wind and water or by transported rhizome fragments. In late fall and winter, the above-ground portions of Common Reed die and turn straw-colored, but remain erect, and it is challenging to walk through a dense Common Reed patch at almost any time of year.

HABITAT: Common Reed is found in tidal freshwater to brackish marshes. Newly disturbed, sunny areas such as dredge disposal sites and spoil piles along ditches are prime areas that are often quickly colonized by Common Reed. It is not limited to tidal areas and is more widely distributed in nontidal freshwater wetlands.

CONFUSED WITH: In higher salinity areas, no other tall grass resembles Common Reed. In freshwater wetlands, some of the Plume grasses (several *Saccharum* species) may superficially resemble Common Reed. Common Reed can be mistaken for another invasive, Giant Reed (*Arundo donax*), but this is less common. As the common name indicates, Giant Reed looks like Common Reed on steroids.

WILDLIFE/ECOLOGICAL VALUE: As an invasive, Common Reed can supplant the native flora and reduce local biodiversity. In the Bay it is assumed to provide inferior wildlife habitat in comparison with more diverse wetland communities. Since it forms dense stands and produces copious amounts of leaf and stem litter, it has been postulated that Common Reed can alter localized sedimentation patterns and raise marsh elevations. Due to the extensive network of rhizomes, it can help bind the soil and stabilize shorelines.

HUMAN USES: In the Bay, hunters commonly use Common Reed to construct duck blinds. Common Reed is often planted in wetlands constructed for wastewater treatment. Native Americans have reportedly used Common Reed to make mats, musical instruments, and arrow shafts. In other parts of the world, it is still used in construction as thatch.

A marsh dominated by Salt-marsh Cord Grass, typical of many areas in the Bay.

Cord Grasses, *Spartina* species

It is probably not an exaggeration to say that grasses in the *Spartina* genus are the most important grasses in the marshes of the Chesapeake Bay—and are perhaps the most important of all the plants. Salt-marsh Cord Grass (*Spartina alterniflora*), plays a critical role in substrate stabilization as well as providing detritus for a myriad of microorganisms that are essential for maintaining many Bay and marine species.

DISTINGUISHING FEATURES: Cord Grasses often form large, conspicuous stands at many places in the Bay. The scientific name, *Spartina*, and the common name, Cord Grass, are derived from the arrangement of the flowers on their stalks, a pattern resembling woven cord. This feature and their preference for brackish and even saline waters make them one of the easiest groups of grasses to recognize. Their adaptation to salt is remarkable; Salt-marsh Cord Grass, for example, can secrete salt through its leaves. Plants are often encrusted with salt.

1. Salt-marsh Cord Grass (*Spartina alterniflora*). Leaves often reach a height of 5 ft., overtopped by the flowering stems, although the size of the plants varies considerably, depending on availability of nutrients. The inconspicuous green flowers appear in the summer; grains are produced in the late fall. This is the best-known and most abundant of all Bay grasses.
2. Salt-meadow Cord Grass (*Spartina patens*). This is the smallest, seldom more than 3 ft. tall, and the most wiry Cord Grass. It often forms dense,

A meadow of Salt-meadow Cord Grass. The braided-cord appearance of the flowering stem in the female phase of flowering (*right*). Although they appear at different times, the flowers contain both sexes.

Cord Grasses (continued)

meadow-like stands in saline soils of marshes, but can also be found on the edge of beaches and occasionally on sand dunes.

3. Big Cord Grass (*Spartina cynosuroides*). Of the three Cord Grasses in the Bay, this is the largest, reaching 15 ft. tall, with large leaves possessing sharp, saw-like teeth. Compared with the other two species, Big Cord Grass favors a less-saline habitat. It is also the only Cord Grass bearing flowers with branches at sharp right angles to the main axis. Flowering branches are pressed tight against the stem in all the other Cord Grasses.

CONFUSED WITH: When flowering and fruiting, these grasses are easy to distinguish. With experience it is possible to identify any of the three species based on the way the leaf joins the stem.

WILDLIFE/ECOLOGICAL VALUE: It may be hyperbole to say that the Bay ecosystem in many places is dependent on Salt-marsh Cord Grass, but it would not be totally wrong. Extensive research on the role of this species clearly indicates it is vital to Bay waters.

HUMAN USES: There are few human uses for these plants although *S. alterniflora* is available commercially for wetland restoration.

A dense stand of Big Cord Grass in fruit.

The dark-green color of Needle Rush gives a black appearance to marshes, a feature especially evident in the winter. A fruiting plant (*opposite*). The brown capsules are barely visible among the dense stems.

Rushes, *Juncus* species

Large areas of the Chesapeake Bay are invested with species of rush. These grass-like plants are diverse; about 10 species can be found in Bay wetlands. We have chosen three species as examples of the diversity in form and habitat of Bay rushes: Needle Rush, or Black Needle Rush (*Juncus roemarianus*) is the most widespread and perhaps the best known; Soft-stem Rush (*Juncus effuses*) is one of the most common rushes in eastern North America; and Creeping Rush (*Juncus repens*) is the least rush-like of rushes.

CHARACTERISTICS OF RUSHES: Along with members of the grass family (Poaceae) and sedge family (Cyperaceae), rushes are graminoids; that is, grass-like plants. However, in many species of rush there is nothing resembling typical leaves; instead, the leaves are small, inconspicuous structures at the base of the stems. Flowers are small and easily overlooked. Unlike the other graminoids, rushes produce a many-seeded fruit. The seeds are very small.

1. Needle Rush. Anyone who has spent time in Bay salt marshes gets the point about Needle Rush—literally. The tip of the stem is sharp and hard, and botanists are ready targets. To use comic-book terminology, this is the Hulk of the Bay's rushes, with tough, long rhizomes and equally tough leaves that can be 4 ft. tall. Unlike the other rushes treated here, Needle Rush produces flowers on stalks much shorter than the tall stems. These are difficult to find amid the surrounding protective stems.
2. Soft-stem Rush. This is one of the most common species of rush through much of North America. The stems, up to 4 ft. tall, are indeed soft. It

flowers and fruits about the same time as Needle Rush, in early summer to midsummer. Unlike Needle Rush, it forms very dense clumps and does not have a creeping rootstock. Limited to freshwater.

3. Creeping Rush. This is the least rush-like of any of our rushes because it has what appear as typical leaves. As the common name states, this plant creeps along mud, rooting along the stems. The leaves are 0.5 in. long and flat. Flowers are produced in heads. Creeping Rush is the most aquatic of our rushes and can grow as a submergent. It reaches its northern limit in the Bay. It occurs only in freshwater.

HABITAT: Most rushes are plants of wet areas. Only a few will tolerate salinity, most notably, Needle Rush.

CONFUSED WITH: The many species of rush found in the region are mainly determined on technical characteristics of the fruits and leaf sheaths, and even of the seeds.

WILDLIFE/ECOLOGICAL VALUE: Needle Rush is a keystone species in salt marshes along the Atlantic and Gulf Coasts. It traps sediment and adds to the biomass, which in turn creates detritus for microorganisms that are consumed by small animals. Such habitats are havens for small fish and other creatures. Soft-stem Rush provides food and cover for waterbirds.

HUMAN USES: Rushes can be used to weave baskets and mats. Needle Rush is sometimes planted for wetland restoration.

Soft-stem Rush in fruit. The three-sided capsule contains hundreds of small seeds.

Creeping Rush. The overall appearance is very different from the other species, but the fruiting structures, grey clusters in lower right, readily link this species with the Rush genus.

A dense stand of Salt Grass with developing fruits. The sexes in this species are segregated on separate plants. Female stands, like the one in the photo, usually inhabit areas higher in nutrients than those where male plants are found.

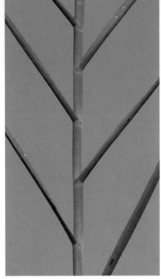

Salt Grass can easily be mistaken for Bermuda Grass (*Cynodon dactylon*), at least in the vegetative state. However, Bermuda Grass has short hairs at the juncture of the leaf and stem (*left*); Salt Grass lacks these (*right*). Salt Grass has a brown base of the leaf, which is not found in Bermuda Grass.

Salt Grass, *Distichlis spicata*

A meadow of Salt Grass in midsummer resembles the children's game pick-up-sticks: stems are lying helter-skelter, some stems flattened, some upright. No doubt this appearance of disarray is due to the frequent overwash that these habitats experience at storm tides. Salt Grass is well adapted both to this disturbance and to the high salinity of the soil.

DISTINGUISHING FEATURES: Wiry, tough grass with narrow leaves and extensive rhizomes, seldom more than 2 ft. tall. Flowers are produced in the early summer; grains develop in late summer and early fall. The female flowers are light pink.

HABITAT: Restricted to salt marshes, where it can form extensive stands.

CONFUSED WITH: Without the flowering or fruiting heads, Salt Grass can be confused with other grasses with narrow leaves and stems. Bermuda Grass (*Cynodon dactylon*) is easily mistaken for Salt Grass in the vegetative state. This is a problem because Bermuda Grass can invade the edges of salt meadows. However, the two species are readily distinguished by the presence or absence of hairs at the juncture of the leaf and stem.

WILDLIFE/ECOLOGICAL VALUE: This plant is an important element of salt marshes. It consolidates the substrate, even with flooding and tides.

HUMAN USES: Formerly a source of fodder for cattle.

A marsh dominated by Square-stem Spike Rush (*opposite*). A flowering stalk showing the four-angled stem (*right*). Fruits are very dark in this species (*below*).

Spike Rushes, *Eleocharis* species

These are unobtrusive plants of wetlands with a charm all their own. In fact, the scientific name means "gracing a marsh," an appropriate name for these grass-like plants. About 25 species of spike rush can be found in Bay waters. We treat only three here: Square-stem Spike Rush (*Eleocharis quadrangulata*); Hair-like Spike Rush (*Eleocharis acicularis*); and Small Spike Rush (*Eleocharis parvula*).

GENERAL FEATURES OF THE GENUS: These rushes lack typical leaves. Instead, the stem is the organ of photosynthesis, and it also produces the flowers at its tip. Flowers are in a distinct spiral arrangement and are small and easily overlooked. Fruits are hard and one-seeded. Most species have a specialized structure on the tip of the fruit, the tubercle, that is spongy and may help buoy the fruit as a means of water dispersal.

1. Square-stem Spike Rush. This is the only species of spike rush in the Chesapeake Bay flora that has square stems and terminal flowering heads that are equal in width to the stem.
2. Hair-like Spike Rush. Thin, hair-like stems and a mat-forming behavior are features of this widespread species of freshwater rush. As all of the *Eleocharis* species, it has flowers clustered at the top of the stems.
3. Small Spike Rush. This is one of a handful of these rushes that live in brackish or salt marshes. Unlike the other species considered here, Small Spike Rush forms tufts.

71

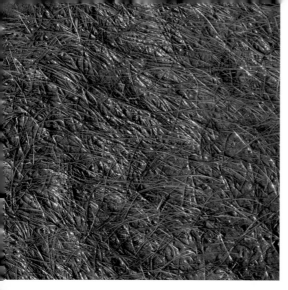

(*Left*) A mat of Hair-like Spike Rush on a mudbank in a tidal river.

(*Below*) Flowering stems of Hair-like Spike Rush.

Spike Rushes (continued)

DISTINGUISHING FEATURES: Small Spike Rush is the only dwarf spike rush to be found in brackish and saline marshes.

HABITAT: All spike rushes are wetland plants. Most of those in the Bay are freshwater plants.

CONFUSED WITH: Spike rushes have terminal, spirally arranged flowers. Within the species it can be difficult to determine among them. The most distinctive is the Square-stem Spike Rush. The other species are often difficult to distinguish because the criteria used to differentiate them are technical characteristics of fruits, tubercles, and bristles that surround the fruit.

WILDLIFE/ECOLOGICAL VALUE: Spike rushes are an important food source for wildlife. Some species, including the Square-stem Spike Rush, are sold for marsh restoration and enhancement. The mat-forming species (e.g., Hair-like Spike Rush) consolidate soil in mudflats and other areas of bare soil.

HUMAN USES: Several species have been used for making mats and weaving. Water Chestnut, the popular Chinese vegetable, is a species of spike rush (*Eleocharis dulcis*). The tubers of some of our native species could also be edible. We have not tried them.

(*Opposite*) Small Spike Rush in a Salt Marsh. The yellowish green stems are a frequent feature of this species.

This specimen has the typical straw color of the species.

A cluster of hundreds of single-seeded fruits of Straw-colored Flatsedge.

Straw-colored Flatsedge, *Cyperus strigosus*

This genus gives its name to the sedge family (Cyperaceae). The common name, Flatsedge, is descriptive of the way the flowers and fruits are borne in these grass-like plants. Other common names include Galingale and Umbrella Sedge. Like many other members of the family, Flatsedges are often found in wetlands. Only a few species are found in the Bay, however, and we have selected a single species as representative of this group, Straw-colored Flatsedge.

DISTINGUISHING FEATURES OF THE GENUS: What sets these apart from other sedges is the distinct manner in which the flowers and fruits are borne. They are flattened in one plane. Branches with these compressed flowers, however, may be variously arranged in globe-shaped clusters or other configurations.

Flowers are tiny and inconspicuous. The single-seeded fruits are small. In late summer and fall, the plants generally take on a yellow color. Vegetatively, Flatsedge is unremarkable, with leaves having corrugated folds; stems are triangular in cross section.

HABITAT: Straw-colored Flatsedge is a common component of salt marshes, growing with such plants as Salt Grass and glassworts.

CONFUSED WITH: Other members of the sedge family, especially when flowers and fruits are not present.

WILDLIFE/ECOLOGICAL VALUE: The fruits are a likely food for wildlife.

HUMAN USES: None known.

A marsh of Narrow-leaf Cattail in early spring (*opposite*). A fruiting stalk (*left*) shows the separation between the two flower regions. One way to differentiate between these two common species is to think of the letter *A* (for *angustifolia*), signifying apart. The male and female flower stalks have a gap between them.

Cattails, *Typha latifolia* and *Typha angustifolia*

Cattails are one of the best sources of emergency foods and are so nutritious they are eaten at other times as well. These well-known utilitarian plants grace many parts of the Bay, both freshwater and brackish. We here consider the two common species of the Bay, Broad-leaf Cattail (*Typha latifolia*) and Narrow-leaf Cattail (*Typha angustifolia*).

DISTINGUISHING FEATURES: The strap-like leaves of cattails can be 7 ft. or more tall. All the leaves arise from the base of the plant. The flat leaves are spongy and contain mucilage. In the spring, when the plants flower, they produce thousands of flowers on a single flowering stalk. Flowers are arranged on the stalk separately by sex, with the male flowers at the top and the female flowers below. The male flowers produce copious pollen, which is shed in a short time. The female flowers, green in color, are tiny and crowded together, like their mates above, on a thickened axis. Soon little remains of the male flower stalk; it appears dry and white, above the female. The iconic brown cattail is an aggregation of innumerable small fruits that will open in the fall to produce the down that floats in the air and distributes the seeds.

HABITAT: Anywhere there is water, there is likely to be cattail. Narrow-leaf Cattail can tolerate salinity, while Broad-leaf Cattail is a freshwater plant.

CONFUSED WITH: A third species, Southern Cattail (*Typha domingensis*), infrequent in Bay waters, is separated from the other two species by technical characteristics.

A Broad-leaf Cattail marsh with fruiting stalks (*opposite*). The species in flower (*right*). The female and male flower groups are confluent.

Cattails (continued)

WILDLIFE/ECOLOGICAL VALUE: Cattails are hugely important in marshes. Among their many uses, we will mention only that muskrats relish the rhizomes, birds use the down for lining nests, and a diversity of animals live in cattail marshes. These plants also help stabilize shorelines.

HUMAN USES: A book could be written on the uses of cattails. It is one of the few marsh plants—indeed, one of the few wild plants—where all parts can be used. The pollen is nutritious, and since it is produced in large quantities it can be collected and used for food. The female flowering stalk can be boiled and eaten, as can the young, leafy shoots. Rhizomes contain large quantities of edible starch and are easy to prepare. Cattail leaves can be used to make mats and baskets. The mature fruits, when dipped in oil, have even found use as torches. The seeds, too, are reported to be edible, but the innumerable hairs curb our enthusiasm.

Five-angled Dodder smothering young Red Maples at the edge of a marsh.

Dodders, *Cuscuta* species

Dodders blanket their hosts with twining, leafless orange stems, looking not unlike a mass of discarded spaghetti haphazardly tossed onto a shrub. Not being dependent on chlorophyll to produce their food, they are the only nongreen plants in Bay waters; rather, dodders are parasitic: they depend upon their hosts for nutrients. Several species of dodders are found in Bay wetlands.

DISTINGUISHING FEATURES OF THE GENUS: The yellow or orange leafless, twining stems parasitize their hosts through modified roots that form peg-like intrusions into the host tissue. Dodder plants often form large, colorful masses of tangled stems on their hosts. Small, white flowers are borne in the summer, developing into a three- or four-seeded capsule. The very hard seeds require the seed coat to be broken for germination.

HABITAT: Because the hard seed coat needs abrasion, dodders are often found along streams or in tidal regions where water movement can abrade the seed surface. They prefer open, sunny areas and will grow on a great diversity of hosts.

SPECIES CHARACTERISTICS: We have selected two of the five species as examples of the genus in Bay habitats.

1. Five-angled Dodder (*Cuscuta pentagona*). First described from Norfolk, Virginia, this species is sometimes included with Field Dodder, *Cuscuta campestris*. The common name accurately describes the overall shape of

Collared Dodder, *Cuscuta indecora*, parasitizing Marsh Elder (*opposite*). The dead branches are likely a result of parasitism. Collared Dodder flowers have distinctive bumps (*left*), which make them glisten, a unique feature among the five Dodder species in the Bay region.

Dodders (continued)

the pentagonal flower. This dodder has an extensive host range and can sometimes be found on marsh plants, where it can produce spectacular mounds of tangled stems.

2. Collared Dodder (*Cuscuta indecora*). In Virginia, found most commonly on Marsh Elder in Cord Grass marshes. It is easily recognized by the distinct, blister-like bumps on the petals and sepals, which make the surface glisten. This species is sometimes known as Bigseed Dodder.

CONFUSED WITH: Dodders cannot be confused with other plants, although distinguishing one species from another can be difficult for the novice.

WILDLIFE/ECOLOGICAL VALUE: The value of dodders to Bay wildlife is unknown, but studies in other ecosystems have shown that the parasitism by dodders helps regulate populations of host plants.

HUMAN USES: Because of their growth pattern, which forms intimate connections between host and parasite, dodders are also known as Love Vine. This may be the rationale for including dodder (seed?) extracts in so-called male-potency herbal remedies for which there is no documented efficacy. We have used dodder stems to prepare a dye for wool, and samples have remained color fast for more than five years.

Orache on a low, sandy beach in the Bay (*opposite*). The spreading stems are evident. The leaves of this species have a distinct, halberd-like shape at the base, like a double-headed ax.

Orache, *Atriplex patula*

A common component of salt marshes, Orache is also found in weedy areas, particularly those with heavy soils. It is widespread through eastern North America. *Patula* means spreading, an allusion to the clambering activity of the stems.

DISTINGUISHING FEATURES: A spreading annual with succulent stems and leaves. The younger stems and leaves, which are about 5 in. long, are densely covered with mealy, white glands that fall when the leaves mature. These may function as a salt regulator, allowing the plant to survive in saline habitats. Flowers are small and greenish, producing tiny, shiny seeds in the fall.

HABITAT: Orache is commonly found in salt marshes and along beaches. But its weedy adaptations allow it also to survive in disturbed areas such as margins of piers and embankments.

CONFUSED WITH: The leaves of Orache can resemble those of the Halberd-leaved Tearthumb, but it is easily distinguished by the lack of armor.

WILDLIFE/ECOLOGICAL VALUE: None known.

HUMAN USES: The leaves are edible and good when collected young. Seeds are also edible. Several species of this genus are grown in saline deserts for dune stabilization.

Thin branches and fleshy, thickened leaves are a feature of this aster (*opposite*). Flowering heads of Salt-marsh Aster show the two types of flowers, the light blue outer flowers and the tubular, yellow, inner flowers.

Salt-marsh Aster, *Symphyotrichum tenuifolium*

White is not a common color in salt marshes in the late summer, so the Salt-marsh Aster, with its light, whitish tints, stands out. Like most other plants in salt marshes, this relative of Dandelion and Goldenrod has succulent leaves. Also known as *Aster tenuifolium*.

DISTINGUISHING FEATURES: Salt-marsh Aster is a weak-stemmed perennial, reaching a height of 3 ft. The leaves are fleshy, a feature shared with several other salt marsh species. In midsummer flowers appear. Like other daisies, this species has heads comprised of two types of flowers in a single head. The central region of the head has tubular yellow flowers, while those along the margin have a broad, very light, whitish-blue extension.

HABITAT: Restricted to salt marshes, often with Salt Grass (*Distichlis spicata*).

CONFUSED WITH: An annual species, Annual Salt-marsh Aster (*Symphyotrichum subulatum*), grows in similar habitats and can be distinguished from the perennial species by its considerably smaller outer flowers of the head, as well as its annual habit.

WILDLIFE/ECOLOGICAL VALUE: None noted.

HUMAN USES: None noted.

Slender Marsh Pink (*opposite*) grows in brackish marshes in full sun, usually as an isolated individual. Perennial Sea Pink (*Sabatia dodecandra*), like Slender Marsh Pink, has green markings at the base of its petals, outlined in red.

Sea Pinks, species of the genus *Sabatia*

These belong to the gentian family, a family well known for its beautiful flowers. Slender Marsh Pink (*Sabatia campanulata*) with its beautiful flowers of bright pink, reflects well on its family and displays an unusual color for salt marshes in midsummer.

DISTINGUISHING FEATURES: The delicate stems and narrow leaves along with the five-parted flower make Slender Marsh Pink easy to identify. Late in summer and early autumn a many-seeded capsule is produced.

HABITAT: The Sea Pinks considered here occupy brackish to salt marshes.

CONFUSED WITH: Annual Sea Pink (*Sabatia stellaris*) is found in the marshes of the Bay and resembles *S. campanulata*, but it is an annual.

WILDLIFE/ECOLOGICAL VALUE: None recorded.

HUMAN USES: Some Sea Pinks have been used as a source of bitter medicine. Other species are grown as ornamentals.

Flowers and buds of White Loosestrife.
The flowers are about 1 in. across.

Purple Loosestrife, at present only an oddity in freshwater portions of the Bay, has tremendous potential for invading natural plant communities. These flowers are about 2 in. across.

White Loosestrife, *Lythrum lineare*

This white-flowered perennial is easily overshadowed by its bolder grass and rush neighbors.

DISTINGUISHING FEATURES: White Loosestrife has narrow leaves in an opposite pattern on delicate, usually much-branched stems. Plants are seldom more than 6 ft. tall. It flowers throughout the summer and produces a small, many-seeded capsule at the end of the growing season. The five-parted flowers are crinkled, a feature it shares with other members of its family, including the commonly planted street tree Crape Myrtle (*Lagerstroemia indica*).

Purple Loosestrife (*Lythrum salicaria*) has been introduced from Eurasia and is now one of the most noxious weeds in freshwater communities throughout eastern North America. It invades marshes and wins out in competition with native plants, resulting in a uniform stand, reducing diversity. The beast at least is beautiful, as this plant has strikingly attractive masses of purple flowers; however, the show cannot mask the extreme damage it inflicts. Millions of dollars are spent every year to control it. Fortunately, at present, it is rare in Bay waters.

HABITAT: White Loosestrife is restricted to brackish marshes.

CONFUSED WITH: Nothing in a salt marsh resembles White Loosestrife.

WILDLIFE/ECOLOGICAL VALUE: None known.

HUMAN USES: None known.

A familiar sight in autumn all around the Bay, a Groundsel Tree in flower at the margin of a Needle Rush marsh.

Clusters of female flowers of Groundsel Tree are shown below
(*left*), with male flowers on the right. Fruits (*right*) resemble
those of Common Dandelion (*Taraxacum officinale*).

Groundsel Tree, *Baccharis halimifolia*

Groundsel Tree is not really a tree despite its common name; rather, it is a large shrub—the most abundant and widespread of the large shrubs in the Chesapeake Bay region. Groundsel is thought to refer to a related group of plants in the genus *Senecio*, known in British English as groundsel. This evergreen is readily recognized any season of the year.

DISTINGUISHING FEATURES: A much-branched, vigorous shrub, up to 10 ft. tall, with thick leaves about 2.5 in. long, and green stems. Plants are unisexual; that is, there are male and female plants. Flowers are very small and clustered into heads. Female flowers are white, male flowers yellow, and flowering shrubs can thus be distinguished at a distance. The small, single-seeded fruits are borne late in the autumn, with long, silky hairs that aid in their dispersal. Many of the leaves are retained through the winter.

HABITAT: A native component of salt marshes, this shrub has a very broad ecological amplitude. Unlike other shrubs in Bay salt marshes, Groundsel Tree spreads aggressively into old fields and waste areas.

CONFUSED WITH: Marsh Elder (*Iva frutescens*) often grows with Groundsel Tree and superficially may resemble it. See Marsh Elder.

WILDLIFE/ECOLOGICAL VALUE: Groundsel Tree has been introduced to Europe, where it is considered invasive.

HUMAN USES: None recorded for the Bay region.

93

The dramatic flowers of Seashore Mallow in late summer. The flowers are about 5 in. in diameter.

Mallows, *Kosteletzkya virginica* and *Hibiscus moscheutos*

Our two native species of mallow are among the largest and showiest flowers of any of our native plants. Seashore Mallow is a common component of brackish marshes in the Chesapeake Bay watershed. Marsh Hibiscus is a closely related species.

DISTINGUISHING FEATURES: Seashore Mallow is a semishrub found in tidal situations. It can have from a few to many branches, has conspicuous pink flowers, and alternate, simple leaves. Like other members of this group, the veins in the leaves are arranged like the palm of a hand. This species grows to a height of up to 6 ft. The fruit is a capsule with five hard, black seeds.

HABITAT: Commonly found in full sun in tidal areas from freshwater to brackish.

CONFUSED WITH: Marsh Hibiscus, close relative of Seashore Mallow, can be found with Seashore Mallow, but the latter has smaller flowers that are generally pink, while Marsh Hibiscus, a taller plant, has larger, white flowers.

WILDLIFE/ECOLOGICAL VALUE: The showy flowers of Seashore Mallow are attractive to hummingbirds.

HUMAN USES: Seashore Mallow is grown on a small scale as an ornamental. Natural oils extracted from the seeds of Seashore Mallow are being evaluated as a potential source of biodiesel fuel. In northern China, this species is being tested as a possible saline-tolerant crop to improve soil conditions and help establish an ecologically friendly saline-farming industry.

A common winter scene in Bay salt marshes—a stand of Marsh Elder at the margin of a Salt-marsh Cord Grass community (*opposite*). Marsh Elder commonly grows with Groundsel Tree, but unlike the latter has inconspicuous flowers, borne in small, dense heads.

Marsh Elder, *Iva frutescens*

Marsh Elder is one of the most common and abundant species in salt marshes. The flowers are tiny, unattractive, and apparently wind-pollinated. The common name seems to come from a purported resemblance to true Elder (*Sambucus canadensis*).

DISTINGUISHING FEATURES: Marsh Elder is a much-branched shrub, seldom more than 10 ft. tall. On any given plant, most of the leaves will be arranged in an opposite manner. These are fleshy (at least when young) and up to 1.2 in. long, with regular teeth. Flowers are produced in the summer, but are easily overlooked because they are small and in compact heads on the upper branches of the shrub. This is the latest-flowering shrub of our salt marshes, with flowers frequently produced in the winter. The fruits are tiny and one-seeded.

HABITAT: Dense stands of Marsh Elder can be found at the edge of salt marshes, where it commonly grows with Groundsel Tree on the part of the marsh that is slightly higher than the habitat of Salt-marsh Cord Grass. Unlike some other salt-marsh species, Marsh Elder frequently occupies disturbed areas where marshes have been filled.

CONFUSED WITH: Groundsel Tree and Marsh Elder often grow together, forming an assemblage known as a salt-shrub community. The plants can be confused with one another, but they can be distinguished by growth patterns: Marsh Elder is more compact than Groundsel Tree. Leaves are always arranged in an alternate pattern on Groundsel Tree, while those on Marsh Elder are opposite. Groundsel Tree

On the left are Marsh Elder leaves (*top row*) compared with Groundsel Tree leaves (*bottom row*). Marsh Elder has very small fruits—the size of rice grains (*right*).

Marsh Elder (continued)

leaves have a scurfy white surface, giving the shrub an overall grey appearance. The fruits are strikingly different. See Groundsel Tree.

WILDLIFE/ECOLOGICAL VALUE: Because it will grow in saline areas, Marsh Elder is commercially available for habitat improvement.

HUMAN USES: The fruits of other species in the genus have been used as food; however, we have found no information on Marsh Elder.

Sea Oxeye, with characteristic bright-yellow flowers and grey-green leaves (*at left*).

A bumblebee feeding on the flowers of Sea Oxeye. Like its relative the Dandelion, Sea Oxeye has small flowers clustered in heads, giving the appearance of a large, single flower.

Sea Oxeye, *Borrichia frutescens*

Sea Oxeye brightens saline mudflats with its yellow, daisy-like flowers in midsummer.

DISTINGUISHING FEATURES: Sea Oxeye, a small shrub with stiff stems, seldom reaches 2.5 ft. tall. It has fleshy, succulent leaves. The yellow flowers are produced from mid to late summer and contrast with the grey-green leaves and stems. Fruits are small and released in the autumn and winter, which leaves the receptacles to bleach white in the sun and persist to the next season.

HABITAT: Sea Oxeye is a true halophyte and frequently forms large, uniform stands at the edge of salt marshes.

CONFUSED WITH: There are numerous yellow-flowered plants in Bay marshes, but few grow in salt marshes or flower at the same time as Sea Oxeye.

WILDLIFE/ECOLOGICAL VALUE: The usually dense stands provide cover for wildlife.

HUMAN USES: Sometimes used as a garden subject.

PLANTS OF

Freshwater Habitats

American Lotus fruit. The individual seeds are the same size as Chinquapin, a dwarf native chestnut (*Castanea pumila*), hence one of the common names, Water Chinquapin.

American Lotus, *Nelumbo lutea*

Spectacular leaves and stunning flowers characterize this queen of all our water lilies. With leaves up to 5 ft. across and flowers as big as dinner plates, this aquatic plant is a real eye-catcher. The genus *Nelumbo* comprises two similar species: this widespread North American plant, known by a variety of common names, and the pink Sacred Lotus (*Nelumbo nucifera*), native to Asia and iconic in Buddhism and Hinduism.

DISTINGUISHING FEATURES: The huge, slightly funnel-shaped leaves are unique. This is our only water lily that has the leaf stalk in the middle of the leaf, forming an umbrella-like structure. Flowers are borne separately on long stalks, usually at or above the level of the tallest leaves. Leaf stalks, like other parts of the plant, contain a milky latex. Flowering begins in midsummer, and by late summer and early fall the unique fruits are produced.

The young fruits are frequently collected and sold for dried floral displays. American Lotus dies back in the winter, with little evidence of its presence save for an occasional fruit stalk. The extremely hard seeds can remain viable for hundreds of years.

These two flowers of American Lotus have been open for more than a day, as evidenced by the falling of the male flower parts, the stamens.

HABITAT: Shallow, still water in freshwater tidal marshes. The population dynamics are poorly understood: one year there is a flourishing population, the next season little evidence it ever existed.

WILDLIFE/ECOLOGICAL VALUE: Important food source for animals. It also provides habitat for invertebrates.

HUMAN USES: The seeds are edible and can be eaten raw. They soon become refractory, after which they can be ground into flour. Native Americans used the dried seeds to make necklaces. The leaves are reported to be edible, but we have not tried them.

Duckweeds, species of the Lemnaceae

The casual observer would likely consider this group to be little more than pond scum. They are the tiniest flowering plants in the Bay; several could fit under a fingernail. Not only are they the smallest flowering plants in the Chesapeake, they are also the only representative of a group of aquatic plants, free-floating, found in these waters. In other words, because they are not rooted in the substrate, duckweeds are at the whims of the winds and tides, which is why they are often found pushed against a shoreline or stranded on mud.

DISTINGUISHING FEATURES: Duckweeds are appropriately named: they ride on the surface of the water like ducks. They also are a favored food of some waterfowl. Water Flaxseed has several roots per leaf, duckweed only one. Fascinating flowers are produced, but seldom seen. A bouquet of dozens could fit inside a drinking straw. Seeds are produced, but most reproduction is asexual, by budding. All of the duckweeds exhibit this behavior, and it is common to find a mother plant with a daughter plant, that daughter plant with a daughter plant, and so on. As winter approaches, the plants submerge, resurfacing in the spring.

A family reunion. Three different groups of Duckweeds crowd together in this spread (*left*). The larger ones, with the round leaves, are Water Flaxseed (*Spirodela polyrhiza*); the oval-shaped plants, many of them in their blackish fall color, are Duckweeds (species of the genus *Lemna*); and what appear as tiny green dots are Water-meal (species of the genus *Wolffia*). Individual Water-meal plants (*right*), each about the size of a pinhead. Water-meal are the smallest flowering plants anywhere.

HABITAT: The surface of freshwater.

CONFUSED WITH: A group of moss-like plants, the genera *Riccia* and *Ricciocarpus*, are also free-floating, but unlike the duckweeds they are lobed and have a dark undersurface.

WILDLIFE/ECOLOGICAL VALUE: Important food for some waterfowl.

HUMAN USES: Duckweeds have been used to treat wastewater.

Golden Club. The upper surfaces of the leaves are strongly water repellant (*opposite*), while the undersurface attracts water—a common feature in floating-leaf plants to aid in positioning for photosynthesis. The yellow male stamens are evident in the photo. The greenish part of the flower is the female portion.

Golden Club, *Orontium aquaticum*

Chesapeake Bay wetlands glow with a diversity of yellow flowers in the late summer. Such displays are much less frequent in the spring, but one exception is Golden Club, a true aquatic plant that flowers in early spring.

DISTINGUISHING FEATURES: From sturdy rootstocks, the leaves, 6 in. long, arise each spring, followed shortly by the bright yellow flowers positioned on specialized stems that ensure the flowers are near but not in the water. The striking yellow flower stalks are one of the first aquatic and wetland plants to blossom in the early spring, just prior to Southern Blue Flag Iris, which sometimes shares the marsh with Golden Club. Snow-white in color, the portion below the yellow flowering section is especially buoyant, ensuring the flowers are above water, where the pollinators, usually flies, can visit them. The fleshy, blue-green fruit appears in summer.

HABITAT: Shallow freshwater throughout the Bay.

CONFUSED WITH: Some leaves of Golden Club may be the same size as Arrow Arum (*Peltandra virginica*), though the venation is different and Golden Club has unlobed leaves.

WILDLIFE/ECOLOGICAL VALUE: Unknown.

HUMAN USES: Unknown.

White Water Lily, *Nymphaea odorata*

This common aquatic plant graces many Bay waters, but seldom in areas more than 6.5 ft. deep. It is less frequent than the Yellow Pond Lily and, vegetatively, is sometimes confused with it.

DISTINGUISHING FEATURES: Arising from vigorous rhizomes anchored in the mud, White Water Lily sends up leaves on long stalks to float on the surface. Leaves have an overall round shape, about 1.5 ft. in diameter. The architecture of the leaf has exquisite adaptations reflecting the stress of life in two different worlds. Externally, the leaf is split in the middle, which allows the two halves some independent movement when disturbed. Internally there are large air spaces and the botanical equivalent of girders, giving the leaf strength without weight, yielding flexibility against the stresses of wind, rain, and turbulent water. Flowers are single, on long flexuous stalks. They open in full sun, when they are visited by a diversity of insects. Insects are often trapped when the flowers close in the afternoon. Flowers are white and fragrant, the white petals contrasting with the bright yellow of the male floral parts, the stamens.

Unlike the other Bay water lilies (American Lotus and Yellow Pond Lily), this species exploits both the upper and the nether worlds for reproduction. Flowers are pollinated by flying insects, yet fruits develop underwater. When mature, the seeds are released with an appendage that traps air so they can float on the surface and be dispersed by water currents. The appendage decays, and the seeds sink to the bottom.

(*Opposite*) The leaves of White Water Lily are evenly distributed on the water surface to maximize capture of light. The large, fragrant flowers open in the morning and close in the afternoon or when cloudy.

White Water Lily showing the distinct lobes or auricles where the leaf is divided. Like Golden Club and other aquatic plants with floating leaves, the upper leaf surface repels water and the lower surface attracts water.

HABITAT: Like our other water lilies, this is a freshwater plant. All three water lilies may be found growing together. Of the three, White Water Lily grows in the deepest water. In contrast to the other two, this species is essentially restricted to its aquatic realm, whereas Yellow Pond Lily and American Lotus can grow on exposed wet soil.

CONFUSED WITH: The leaves can look like those of the Yellow Pond Lily. However, the presence of the ear-like lobe at the edge of the two margins readily identifies White Water Lily.

WILDLIFE/ECOLOGICAL VALUE: A host of invertebrates can be found on the underside of leaves and on leaf stalks. Leaves are often extensively tunneled by insects.

HUMAN USES: White Water Lily has limited human uses. There are reports of floral buds being used as food, but in our experience the taste is enough to gag a maggot.

Flowers of Yellow Pond Lily. These are visited by a diversity of insects.

Yellow Pond Lily, *Nuphar lutea*

Also known as Cow Lily and Spatterdock; in fact, this plant like so many widely distributed plants has a myriad common names. Of our three native water lilies in the Bay, this is the most frequent. It also forms the most extensive stands.

DISTINGUISHING FEATURES: This can be both a floating-leaf and a rooted emergent aquatic plant. It arises from a thick, starchy rhizome, with broadly heart-shaped leaves up to 2.5 ft. long, on leaf stalks growing up from the base of the plant. Populations of both floating-leaf and emergent leaf populations are common in freshwater of the Bay. Solitary yellow flowers also arise from the base of the plant. These are about the size of a half dollar, yellow, with green outer parts. The flowering season is long, from spring until frost. Fruits are green when mature, about the size of a plum, and filled with hard, brown seeds in a pasty matrix. Unlike the White Water Lily, this species develops its fruits out of the water.

HABITAT: Restricted to freshwater habitats, where it can form large plants at the edge of tidal marshes. One of the colorful common names is Water Collard, which is a good description of this growth form. On the other hand, extensive stands of Yellow Pond Lily grow submerged, with leaves floating on the water. Plants cannot prosper in water deeper than 6.5 ft.

CONFUSED WITH: The floating leaf form can be confused with White Water Lily, as both have the same general shape. Yellow Pond Lily lacks lobes at the margin of the leaf (see White Water Lily). When growing as an emergent, the leaves resemble

Yellow Pond Lily at low tide in a freshwater marsh. In this habitat the leaves are erect; when the plant grows in deeper standing water, the leaves float.

those of Water Arum, though the pattern of leaf veins is different (see Arrow Arum).

WILDLIFE/ECOLOGICAL VALUE: The massive underwater rootstocks (rhizomes) are frequently dug by muskrats. On muddy tidal flats, the rootstocks stabilize the substrate. Floating leaves provide cover for fish.

HUMAN USES: The seeds are edible. Roasted, their taste is pleasant.

On the right are the dense younger branches of the plant; those on the left are older. Both growths can be found on the same plant.

Hornwort, *Ceratophyllum demersum*

Hornwort is a remnant of an ancient flora as revealed by modern evolutionary studies. The common name is a literal translation of the scientific name; it references the branched, horn-like leaves.

DISTINGUISHING FEATURES: No roots are produced by Hornwort. This is one of a suite of characteristics that make this a unique plant. Leaves are arranged around the stem and are forked. This species of hornwort is distinguished by the teeth on the margins of the leaf lobes. Flowers are unisexual, though both sexes are borne on the same plant. A true water plant, Hornwort is pollinated underwater. The male flower produces a structure that floats to the surface, opens, and allows the pollen—which has the same specific gravity as water—to gently mosey through the water to the waiting female flower. Fruits are one-seeded and have prominent, horn-like extensions. They are seldom seen, however, and we have found none in Bay waters. Most reproduction is by fragmentation of the plant.

HABITAT: True to its scientific name, this plant is demersed, floating below the surface.

CONFUSED WITH: Several plants in the same habitat can be confused with Hornwort, including Hydrilla, Water Milfoil (species of *Myriophyllum*), and the macroscopic algae known as Stoneworts (species of *Chara* and *Nitella*). However, Hornwort is readily distinguished by its forked leaves; none of the others have such leaves.

WILDLIFE/ECOLOGICAL VALUE: Provides good cover for fish and invertebrates.

HUMAN USES: Sold in the aquarium trade. Sometimes large masses impede water activities like swimming and boating.

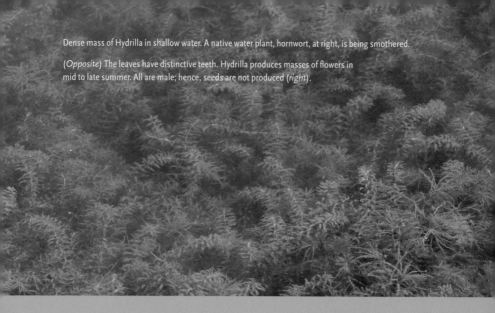

Dense mass of Hydrilla in shallow water. A native water plant, hornwort, at right, is being smothered.

(*Opposite*) The leaves have distinctive teeth. Hydrilla produces masses of flowers in mid to late summer. All are male; hence, seeds are not produced (*right*).

Hydrilla, *Hydrilla verticillata*

Hydrilla is a horrible invasive. It blankets large surfaces of Bay waters and shores. An African native, it was first reported to be in the Bay in the 1980s and has since spread. Its rapid growth (no sexual reproduction is known among Bay Hydrilla) in shallow freshwater crowds out native submergent plants. The decaying plants are carried by wind and tides to the shore, where delicate plants like isoetids face suffocation from the burden of these carcasses. On the other hand, when it grows as a rooted plant, water quality is improved through lower turbidity, which aids fish habitat, and some wildlife managers and fisherman like it. Overall, however, it is a disaster. We have watched with dread seeing Hydrilla spread up Bay rivers, causing damage wherever it is found.

DISTINGUISHING FEATURES: Hydrilla is an annual plant that, like many aquatic plants, overwinters via specialized buds that include storage material and a shoot. When conditions are right in the spring, the plant has a head start, its growing tip and food source being already in place. Leaves are arranged in whorls of five. Flowers appear in midsummer, but the plants are sterile. No seed is produced. Reproduction is both by winter buds (turions) and by fragmentation. Pieces of the plant break off, float away, and can establish in new areas.

114

HABITAT: Hydrilla does not tolerate salinity; it is found only in freshwater.

CONFUSED WITH: Waterweed (*Elodea canadensis*), which looks so similar that the presence of Hydrilla was at first undetermined; it was assumed to be the native Waterweed. However, Waterweed does not have teeth on the margins of the leaves.

HUMAN USES: Millions of dollars are spent every year to control this weed.

Southern Water Nymph, *Najas guadelupensis*

Unlike the attractive water nymphs of Greek mythology, the eponymous *Najas* species are easily overlooked and unremarkable. They spend their entire life underwater, largely unseen.

DISTINGUISHING FEATURES: A common, widespread plant of freshwater it has oppositely arranged narrow, flat leaves about 0.8 in. long. Plants in Bay waters are often covered with epiphytic algae, which mask the deep green color of the leaves with a brown coating. The unisexual flowers are frequent, but so tiny they, like the fruits, are easily overlooked.

HABITAT: In shallow to deep water of tidal rivers; also able to survive in shallow, muddy waters adjacent to marshes.

CONFUSED WITH: A coterie of plants share the general aspect of Southern Water Nymph. Hydrilla is similar in habit but has stiff leaves in a whorled arrangement. Some macrophytic algae such as the Stoneworts (*Chara* and *Nitella* species) resemble Southern Water Nymph, but they have much thinner, brittle, leaf-like structures.

WILDLIFE/ECOLOGICAL VALUE: Ducks and other waterfowl feed on the plants and seeds.

HUMAN USES: Large populations of Southern Water Nymph can interfere with boating and other water activities.

(*Opposite*) Dwarf Sagittaria can form almost uniform stands on exposed mud or among marsh plants.

Male flower. Note the pointed leaves.

Dwarf Sagittaria, *Sagittaria subulata*

No common name is common for this plant. We have adopted Dwarf Sagittaria. Other so-called common names are Hudson Sagittaria (because it is found in the upper tidal zones of that river) and Awl-leaf Arrowleaf, a particularly confusing name since this species does not have arrow-shaped leaves. *Subulate* means awl-shaped, an apt description for the tips of the leaves. But these days, do most people know what an awl is?

DISTINGUISHING FEATURES: These are small, rosette-forming plants, less than 2 in. tall, with pointed leaves. Flowers are typical of the genus, having three white petals, showy, but small. Each flower is unisexual, but a single plant usually bears both male and female flowers. Fruits are one-seeded, each female flower producing several. Unlike any other isoetid (see *Isoetes*), this species, like all in the genus, has a milky juice that is evident when the leaves or underground stems connecting the plants are broken.

HABITAT: Dwarf Sagittaria forms extensive stands on tidal flats, areas that are completely covered by water with each tide. It is particularly susceptible to smothering by the invasive aquatic weeds Hydrilla and Water Dayflower.

CONFUSED WITH: Other isoetids.

WILDLIFE/ECOLOGICAL VALUE: Important in stabilizing mudflats for colonization by other plants.

HUMAN USES: Sold as an aquarium plant.

Grasswort, *Lilaeopsis chinensis*

The lack of a widely used common name is an indication of how inconspicuous and easily overlooked this diminutive plant is. Nor is its specific epithet any indication that it is an exotic. The great botanist Linnaeus mistakenly thought this humble marsh plant was from the Orient.

DISTINGUISHING FEATURES: The plants are small, about 1 in. tall, from spreading underground stems. Grasswort is one of a guild of plants known as isoetids (see below), but its leaves are unique among isoetids, having a blunt, spatula-like tip. These are not, in fact, true leaves, but rather expanded leaf stalks that function as leaves with transverse walls called septae. Flowers are inconspicuous, 0.1 in. in diameter, with tiny, white petals that develop into a single-seeded fruit.

Isoetids are named in reference to the genus *Isoetes* (quillworts), which they resemble. Though unrelated, these plants have morphological features in common, such as similar, small leaves. They all grow in a rosette manner—that is, leaves form a rosette from the base; and they share a common habitat. Physiologically they are also adapted for this habitat with specialized photosynthesis. In the Bay region, four species of isoetids are often found growing together and are, at first glance, difficult to separate. In addition to Grasswort, this group includes quillworts (species of the genus *Isoetes*), Pipewort (*Eriocaulon parkeri*), and Dwarf Sagittaria (*Sagittaria subulata*).

(*Opposite*) Grasswort forms dense stands on exposed mud or interstitially among marsh plants. The characteristic crosswall separations are evident in some leaves. The plants with pointed leaves are Dwarf Sagittaria.

Flowers and developing fruits.

HABITAT: Grasswort forms dense stands on tidal flats and in brackish marshes, sites susceptible to the invasive plants Hydrilla and Water Dayflower, which blanket and suffocate populations.

WILDLIFE/ECOLOGICAL VALUE: Important in stabilizing mudflats for colonization by other plants.

HUMAN USES: None reported.

(*From left to right*) Flowering Pipewort. The flowers in the tallest stem are open, while those on the other three stems are still in bud (*left*). The flowers appear white because of the fringe of hairs surrounding the tiny flowers (*middle*). The photo at right shows the root's unique, segmented appearance (*right*).

Pipewort, *Eriocaulon parkeri*

Pipewort is one of a guild of small plants, isoetids, with whorled leaves that live in the intertidal zone of freshwater and tidal marshes, areas subject to diurnal flooding. Not only is their morphology distinctive, isoetids also have a specialized photosynthetic mechanism that allows them to produce food at night, carbon being assimilated during the day.

DISTINGUISHING FEATURES OF THE SPECIES: Pipewort is seldom larger than a half dollar. It is overlooked and easily confused with other isoetids (Dwarf Sagittaria, Grasswort, and quillworts) that also grow on tidal mudflats. The flowers are among the smallest of any in the Bay flora, 0.004 in. wide; only duckweeds have smaller flowers. Flowers are clustered into heads. Each flower is bearded with white hair, giving the head an overall white color and the plant another common name, White Buttons. This plant is one of the few in the Bay that can be determined solely on the basis of its roots, which have cross bars that give the white roots a ladder-like appearance.

HABITAT: Pipewort lives in one of the most distinctive habitats of the Bay, fresh-water tidal marshes, where it occupies expanses of mud exposed at low tide.

CONFUSED WITH: It shares the overall general morphology of the other isoetids with which it grows.

WILDLIFE/ECOLOGICAL VALUE: While small, Pipewort helps stabilize mudflats, allowing for the establishment of other plants.

HUMAN USES: None known.

Winter Quillwort showing the grass-like whorled leaves characteristic of all our Quillworts.

Quillworts, *Isoetes* species

No group of Chesapeake Bay plants is more obscure than the quillworts, species of the genus *Isoetes*, despite the diversity of the genus in the Bay's waters. These grass-like plants are part of an assemblage of primitive plants broadly grouped with ferns.

DISTINGUISHING FEATURES OF THE GENUS: Small, seldom more than 5 in. tall, these grass-like, submersed or emergent plants sometimes form dense mats in the intertidal zone. Leaves are produced in a whorled pattern from the rootstock and have a slight groove on the upper surface. In cross section, the leaves have four air chambers. No other aquatic plants in the Bay have whorled leaves with four air chambers that arise from a disc-like rootstock.

TABLE 2 | Types of isoetids found in the Chesapeake Bay

	GRASSWORT	QUILLWORTS	PIPEWORT	DWARF SAGITTARIA
Leaves	Blunt tip, with septa	Pointed tip	Pointed tip	Pointed tip
Flowers	In globe-like cluster	Nonflowering	Tiny, in dense head on long stalk	Relatively large, white, unisexual
Fruits	Single-seeded	No fruits	Tiny, in head	Many seeds
Other	Creeping	Bulb-like rootstock	Segmented roots	Creeping; milky juice

Isoetes are remarkably poorly known. Much is yet to be learned about their distribution, life history, and evolution. In fact, recent studies indicate that the Bay is a center of diversity of these plants. Several recently discovered species are endemic to freshwater tidal margins in Bay rivers.

HABITAT: Entirely freshwater. quillworts have little tolerance of salinity. They grow permanently submersed in intertidal zones or as emergents in shallow water or mud. Widespread but consistently overlooked.

SPECIES CHARACTERISTICS: There is considerable taxonomic confusion in the genus *Isoetes* and species are notoriously difficult to identify. As examples, we have selected two of the approximately six quillworts in the Bay. There are no good common names for these poorly studied plants so we suggest the following:

1. *Isoetes hyemalis*, Winter Quillwort. Emergent or submersed, widespread in the Middle Atlantic states. When emergent, this species can die back to the rootstock during dry periods.
2. *Isoetes mattaponica*, Mattaponi Quillwort. Emergent or submersed, this has a narrow endemic restricted to the Chickahominy, Mattaponi, and Pamunkey Rivers. It is one of the very few narrow endemics of the Chesapeake Bay. Ongoing studies indicate there are additional, undescribed species in the Bay.

CONFUSED WITH: Quillworts are part of a guild of plants of similar architecture known as isoetids (i.e., looking like *Isoetes*). In the Bay there are four genera of isoetids: *Eriocaulon*, *Isoetes*, *Lilaeopsis*, and *Sagittaria* (see table 2). All four can grow together. In addition to being diminutive plants with narrow leaves, they share similar distinctive photosynthetic pathways. *Isoetes*, unlike the other isoetids, lacks flowers.

WILDLIFE/ECOLOGICAL VALUE: Waterfowl eat the starchy rootstocks.

HUMAN USES: Chesapeake Bay quillworts seldom reach a size suitable for collecting, but the rootstocks are a good source of starch.

Mattaponi Quillwort, the only known vascular plant endemic to Bay waters.

The creeping, diminutive Waterwort inhabits mudflats. In the photo opposite, the tiny globe in the upper right is a developing fruit.

Waterwort, *Elatine americana*

This moss-like creature, seldom more than 2.5 in. tall, is one of the smallest plants in freshwater marshes. It forms mats on intertidal mudflats. The best time to find it is at low tide in mid- to late summer.

DISTINGUISHING FEATURES: Opposite leaves and the creeping habit of this plant readily distinguish it from its mud-loving colleagues. Flowers are green, tiny, and easily overlooked, as are the small capsules containing dust-like seeds.

HABITAT: Waterwort lives in one of the most distinctive habitats of the Bay—mudflats at the edge of freshwater marshes.

CONFUSED WITH: Waterwort grows with several isoetids, but it is readily distinguished by leaves on the stem, while all isoetids have leaves arising from the base of the plant.

WILDLIFE/ECOLOGICAL VALUE: Its creeping nature enables Waterwort to stabilize bare mud, which creates a site where propagules of other plants might lodge and become established.

HUMAN USES: We know of no human uses.

(*Left*) Short-bristled Horned-beak Sedge. Fruits are borne individually or in groups of two or three.

(*Right*) Tall Horned-beak Sedge fruit showing the long beak at the top of the one-seeded fruit. Note the bristles, which are twice as long as the fruit—a distinguishing feature of this species.

Beak Sedges, species of *Rhynchospora*

Easily overlooked and even ignored because of their grass-like appearance, beak sedges are common in Bay wetlands. They are one of the largest groups in the sedge family (Cyperaceae). Several of the twenty-five or so species in the genus in Virginia and Maryland are found in or near the Chesapeake Bay. Like many plants, these have conflicting common names. They are frequently called beak rushes; alternatively, beak sedges. We prefer the latter name because it links them with their relatives in the sedge family. Only two species are discussed here; they are representative examples of this important wetland genus.

DISTINGUISHING FEATURES OF THE GENUS: Beak sedges are grass-like in appearance, with long, narrow leaves rising from sheaths that surround the stem. Flowers are grouped into globe-like or cylindrical clusters. A distinguishing feature of the genus is a cap-like structure at the apex of the single-seeded fruit. This is the beak, which gives these plants their common name. The best time to identify beak sedges is in late summer and fall, when the fruits are mature.

1. Tall Horned-beak Sedge, also known as Tall Horned-beak Rush (*Rhynchospora macrostachya*), as the common name implies, can be tall—as tall as 6 ft. The brown fruits form in late summer in globe-shaped groups. Like the Short-bristle Beak Rush, the fruits have a long beak, 0.8 in. long. This species can be found in standing water at the edges of creeks and ponds.
2. Short-bristled Horned-beak Sedge. The descriptive common name of this species is even longer than the scientific name, *Rhynchospora corniculata*,

130

Tall Horned-beak Sedge with mature fruits. This Beak Sedge can grow in standing water.

which literally translates as horned fruit with a horn. In general habit, this species and the one above are similar, but they can readily be separated by the shape of the fruit cluster. In Tall Horned-beak Sedge the flowers are compact; in Short-bristled Horned-beak Sedge they are more diffuse.

HABITAT: Beak sedges are wetland plants, favoring open sunny areas, frequently in standing water. Having little tolerance for saltwater, they are restricted to fresh-water wetlands, where they may form large, conspicuous populations.

CONFUSED WITH: Like other species in the grass, sedge, and rush families, beak sedges at first glance look like nondescript, grass-like plants.

WILDLIFE/ECOLOGICAL VALUE: The fruits of beak sedges are important food for a diversity of wildlife, including waterfowl.

HUMAN USES: None known.

This species has long hairs at the tips of the flowering branches.

Coast Cockspur Grass, *Echinochloa walteri*

Of the many grasses and grass-like plants in freshwater marshes of the Bay, none is more distinct than Coast Cockspur Grass. The cumbersome common name is descriptive of the way the flowers and fruits are presented.

DISTINGUISHING FEATURES: An annual grass, Coast Cockspur Grass flowers in midsummer and produces grains by late summer or early fall. The flowering branches, all containing dozens of individual flowers, have an overall triangular outline.

HABITAT: Freshwater marshes in full sun.

CONFUSED WITH: The several species of this genus in the Bay all can readily be recognized as belonging to the group; Coast Cockspur Grass, however, has hairy leaf sheaths.

WILDLIFE/ECOLOGICAL VALUE: An important food for muskrats and other animals.

HUMAN USES: All species of the genus produce edible grains. We have tried this species; the results were underwhelming.

(*Above*) Japanese Sedge showing the dried male flowers during spring.

(*Left*) Fox Sedge developing fruits in tight small clusters in May.

(*Opposite*) Giant Sedge (*left*). A narrow spike of male flowers peaks above the three clusters of female flowers. Bottlebrush Sedge (*right*). Narrow male flower clusters can be seen above the prominent, drooping female flower clusters.

Sedges, *Carex* species

At first encounter, these sedges are a daunting assemblage of plants for the student of natural history to learn because of the number of species, the need to have mature fruit to facilitate identification, and the number of technical characteristics used to distinguish among species. Even professional botanists often shy away from working with this, the largest genus of plants in eastern North America. But anyone interested in wetlands will encounter numerous species of sedges in the genus *Carex*. A fascinating and diverse group of grass-like plants, they are worthy of note.

There are about 50 sedge species in the Chesapeake Bay. Many of the sedges are frequent and abundant. We have selected six, hoping this will encourage appreciation of sedges. The six are: Japanese Sedge (*Carex kobomugi*); Fox Sedge (*Carex vulpinoidea*); Giant Sedge (*Carex gigantea*); Bottlebrush Sedge (*Carex comosa*); Fringed Sedge (*Carex crinita*); and Cypress Swamp Sedge (*Carex joorii*). For more information, refer to a book or online treatment of regional flora.

DISTINGUISHING FEATURES OF THE GENUS: All species are perennial, either from a thick rootstock or a creeping underground stem. While determining individual species is often tedious, recognizing these grass-like plants as members of the genus *Carex* is simple. The way to determine in the field if a grass-like plant is a sedge is to note the stem. Is it three-sided in cross section? Is there a sac-like envelope around the single-seeded fruit? Is the fruit flat or three-sided? (The latter feature is easily noted by rolling the grain between two fingers.) If the answer to

(*Opposite*) A dense clump of Fringed Sedge with drooping clusters of maturing fruits.

Variation in composition of the mainly female clusters is common in this species.

Sedges (continued)

these three questions is yes, you have a species of *Carex*. Most species form dense clumps, seldom more than 5 ft. tall. Leaves of sedges may be folded, with folds running the length of the leaves. Identification of the characteristics that separate species often requires a hand lens.

SPECIES CHARACTERISTICS: We have arranged these examples using easy-to-observe growth forms of the flowering clusters. Identification requires the use of a hand lens or a technical key.

First we list three with flowering and fruiting stems erect:

1. Japanese Sedge. Our only species with unisexual plants with tightly clustered flowers at the summit of the stem, *Carex kobomugi* was inadvisedly introduced from Japan for dune stabilization and is now considered an invasive species because it displaces native plants. Extensive rhizomes enable rapid spread in sand dunes. Seldom more than 8 in. tall, it flowers and fruits in May. It is limited to southern parts of the Bay.
2. Fox Sedge. This is a common sedge throughout eastern North America. It is found in moist areas such as the margins of swamps and ditches. Fox Sedge is one of the few sedges often abundant in disturbed areas, where it can form dense stands, usually where it is sunny. Leaves are often taller than fruiting stems. Fruits are flat. At the top, near the clustered and sessile flower groups, the stem is rough to the touch, like sandpaper.

Sedges (continued)

3. Giant Sedge. Unlike the other two species with erect flowering and fruiting structures, the sexes in Giant Sedge are borne on separate stalks. Male flowers are on narrow spikes and located above the female clusters. The fruit is sharply three-angled. Giant Sedge, in contrast to many other Bay sedges, can tolerate shade and is often found in swamp forests, where it forms scattered clumps.

Next we list three with flowering and fruiting stems drooping:

1. Bottlebrush Sedge. The common name refers to the appearance of the flowers and fruits. It favors calcareous soils and is most frequent along Bay shores that have marl deposits. Forming robust clumps with stems as tall as 5 ft., this species is characterized by a distinct, yellow-green color. Male and female flowers are produced in separate clusters. Bottlebrush Sedge prefers open sunny areas.

2. Fringed Sedge. This is one of the most common sedges in the United States. Reaching a height of 5 ft., it grows in a dense clump and produces numerous drooping clusters of flowers. Some may be entirely female, with a few male flowers at the bottom; others on the same plant may have mainly female flowers with a few males interspersed. The prominent drooping masses of fruits have made this sedge a candidate for ornamental planting. Fringed Sedge is found in a great diversity of wetland habitats throughout the Bay.

3. Cypress Swamp Sedge. Readily identified by the conspicuous waxy covering of the perigynia and the bristly outline of the fruiting clusters, *Carex joorii* is one of the few Bay sedges to mature late in the season. Typically, this sedge grows about 3.5 ft. tall in scattered, solitary clumps in sunny areas at the edge of marshes and in depressions in swamp forests.

HABITAT: The species included here occur in marshes or swamps of the Bay, with one dune species, the Japanese Sedge, that can tolerate some salinity. Most species flower in the spring and produce fruits in midsummer.

CONFUSED WITH: Sedges, like rushes, are often confused with true grasses.

WILDLIFE/ECOLOGICAL VALUE: Sedges are important components of marsh and stream vegetation. They are the most frequent plants in some communities, providing cover and food for wildlife.

HUMAN USES: Despite the large number of species, there are very few documented human uses of species of *Carex* in eastern North America. Often included in seed mixes for wetland mitigation sites.

Flowers and developing fruit of Southern Wild Rice. Unlike Wild Rice, these are drooping.

Southern Wild Rice, *Zizaniopsis miliacea*

Southern Wild Rice, also known as Cut Grass and Water Millet, is a native perennial grass of freshwater marshes, nontidal and tidal. In the southern portions of its range it can form extensive uniform stands, aggressively spreading by rhizomes.

DISTINGUISHING FEATURES: A tall, nonwoody perennial wetland grass species that reaches heights of up to 10 ft. and forms dense stands at the margins of rivers. The leaves have sharp edges, hence the common name Cutgrass, bestowed by those who have had to hike through dense stands of this species.

HABITAT: Plants are found in a diversity of wetland habitats, including marshes, sloughs, ditches, and margins of swamp forests. In Chesapeake Bay freshwater tidal marshes, Southern Wild Rice becomes a more noticeable component of the low and high marsh communities in mid to late summer, when its stems reach up to 10 ft., towering over broad-leaved herbs that, earlier in the season, dominate the marshes (e.g., Arrow Arum, Pickerel Weed, Yellow Pond Lily).

CONFUSED WITH: Often found growing with Southern Wild Rice is Wild Rice (*Zizania aquatica*), a native annual grass of similar habitats and stature; Wild Rice, however, is an annual with noticeably different reproductive structures.

WILDLIFE/ECOLOGICAL VALUE: The fruits of Southern Wild Rice are of limited importance as food for marsh birds. While the grains are edible, they are small and difficult to harvest, making this an inferior grain to that of Wild Rice.

This species forms dense, almost impenetrable stands along coastal rivers.

HUMAN USES: Southern Wild Rice has very high productivity rates, both above and below ground, and has been used in constructed wetlands for wastewater treatment.

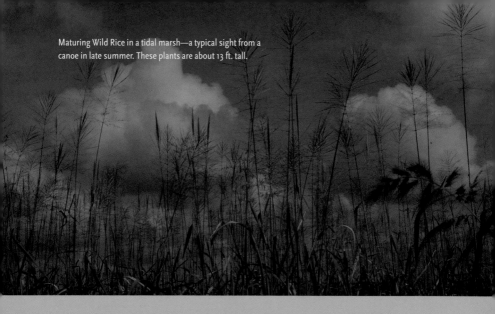

Maturing Wild Rice in a tidal marsh—a typical sight from a canoe in late summer. These plants are about 13 ft. tall.

Wild Rice, *Zizania aquatica*

Wild Rice is the tallest of all Bay marsh grasses. This is a common component of freshwater marshes in our region and across the eastern half of the continent.

DISTINGUISHING FEATURES: Wild Rice is a true aquatic. It begins its life under water. Leaves float until the stem begins to grow. And grow it does: even though an annual plant, it eventually towers over all other marsh vegetation, an adaptation made perhaps for the wind-pollinated flowers, which appear in summer. Adaptation to wind pollination is evident in the dangling male flowers, which release pollen to the breeze. Pollen is then carried to the extended female flowers, which have an air-filter-like configuration to maximize pollen capture. From these flowers develop the characteristic black grains of Wild Rice.

HABITAT: Wild Rice is a predominantly a freshwater plant with only slight tolerance for salinity. It grows in full sun.

CONFUSED WITH: Before its growth spurt, Wild Rice could be confused with other marsh grasses, but in flower and fruit it is distinctive.

WILDLIFE/ECOLOGICAL VALUE: That this is the only Bay plant grown on a commercial scale is a clear measure of its value as food for both wildlife (ducks and other waterfowl) and humans. It is sometimes planted in marshes used by duck hunters.

Flowers and grains of Wild Rice. The female flowers are little more than white puffs extending from the branch (*top, left*), while the more showy males (*top, right*) expose their yellow pollen. Grains are shown in the bottom photo.

HUMAN USES: There is considerable literature on the use of Wild Rice by Native Americans, chiefly for food but also for weaving. Not only the grains but young shoots, too, can be eaten. Like some other grasses, Wild Rice can be popped.

Bur Reed can grow both as an emergent—that is, with its roots in water and its leaves
and flowers out of the water—or as an aquatic plant in running or still water.

(*Opposite*) Bur Reed in flower. The globes of male flowers are above the two groups of female flowers.
Mature fruits are shown in the right photo.

Bur Reed, *Sparganium americanum*

Bur Reed belongs to a coterie of unrelated Bay marsh plants that have strap-shaped leaves. However, the flowers and fruits are distinctive.

DISTINGUISHING FEATURES: A perennial, Bur Reed has long, flexuous spongy leaves which are triangular in cross section, a feature not found in any other Bay plant with strap-shaped leaves. These leaves, in emergent plants, are produced in the same plane and are about 3 ft. long. However, when in flowing water the leaves can be considerably longer. Flowers are produced in the midsummer on a flower stalk in the center of the plant. Flowers are in globe-shaped structures with the female lower and the male above. The many-seeded fruit is round. The tips of the seeds project outward, resembling a bur; hence, the name Bur Reed.

HABITAT: This adaptable plant can grow in running water or as an emergent in a freshwater marsh. In the Bay it is found in both of these habitats.

CONFUSED WITH: See comparisons of marsh plants with strap-shaped leaves.

WILDLIFE/ECOLOGICAL VALUE: The fruits of Bur Reed contain a considerable amount of oil and are an important food for wildlife.

HUMAN USES: None recorded.

The long strap-like leaves of Sweet Flag resemble those of Cattails, but are not as stiff (*left*). The bases of the leaves are characteristically pink.

Sweet Flag, *Acorus calamus*

In other parts of the world, Sweet Flag is valued as a medicinal species. The common name refers to the pleasant fragrance emitted from the plant when the leaves or other parts are broken. Sweet Flag is often first noticed by its distinct fragrance.

DISTINGUISHING FEATURES: Long leaves, up to 6 ft. tall, arise from a tough, pink-tinged rootstock. The leaves are usually transversely corrugated: wavy ridges at right angles to the leaf's long axis. *Flag* is an archaic term for marsh plants with leaves this shape. The leaves die back at the end of the growing season. The flowers of Sweet Flag are miniscule, compacted together on a short axis that arises at a sharp angle from a flowering stalk. Each of the square-shaped flowers is 0.8 in. wide. Sweet Flag produces no fruit because the genetic makeup of the plant renders it sterile.

HABITAT: Frequent in the higher portions of freshwater marshes.

CONFUSED WITH: In Bay waters, several marsh plants have strap-shaped leaves. The following are easily confused: Cattails, Bur Reed, Virginia Iris. Table 3, below, helps to distinguish among them.

The flowering branch contains hundreds of flowers.

WILDLIFE/ECOLOGICAL VALUE: The rootstocks are sometimes harvested by small mammals, apparently for food.

HUMAN USES: Sweet Flag has been used since ancient times for its oil, which is mentioned in the Bible. In colonial times, the rootstocks were collected and boiled in sugar as a candy. There are indications, however, that at least some strains of Sweet Flag could be toxic.

TABLE 3 | Guide to distinguishing between strap-shaped leaves of plants

PLANT	TIP	CROSS SECTION	THIN CLEAR MARGIN	CORRUGATED
Bur Reed	Rounded	Triangular	No	No
Cattail	Pointed Flat	Flat	Yes	Longitudinally
Iris	Pointed Flat	Flat	Yes	Longitudinally
Sweet Flag	Pointed	One side with pointed ridge	Yes	Laterally

Miles of freshwater tidal parts of the Bay are lined with Arrow Arum.
Wild Rice is evident in the vegetation zone next to Arrow Arum.

Arrow Arum, *Peltandra virginica*

The common name comes from the shape of the leaf, a feature shared by several Bay marsh plants. Formerly, Tuckahoe, an aboriginal name, was used, but apparently this has fallen into disfavor.

DISTINGUISHING FEATURES: This is a fleshy plant. The leaves, 3 ft. or more long, arise from a bulb-like base. In Bay waters, it forms large, dense stands at the lower parts of freshwater to slightly brackish marshes—that is, the parts closest to the water. Flowers are seldom seen unless specifically looked for because they are wrapped in an encircling, leaf-like structure and are borne on a fleshy spike. The flowers are small, inconspicuous, and unisexual. As the fruit begins to develop, the stalk grows, forming a gooseneck-like structure that positions the seeds near the water. In the autumn, the seeds detach from the spike and float. Masses of these seeds are often seen along the shorelines of tidal rivers. In winter there is little evidence of Arrow Arum as the plant dies back to its rootstock.

HABITAT: This is a true aquatic plant. It requires standing water or saturated soils and can tolerate some salinity. It is widely distributed throughout eastern North America.

CONFUSED WITH: Superficially similar to other plants with arrow-shaped leaves.

WILDLIFE/ECOLOGICAL VALUE: Waterfowl feed on the seeds. Arrow Arum is a key component of freshwater marshes of the Bay.

A variety of shapes of leaves of arrow-leaf plants. The middle two leaves show extremes of leaf shape in Arrow Arum; on the left is Arrowleaf; on the right, Pickerel Weed. All three of these plants have great plasticity in the shape of the leaves, which depends on water level and water flow.

Arrow Arum (continued)

HUMAN USES: Like other members of this family, Arrow Arum contains large quantities of oxalate crystals, which can cause inflammation of mucous membranes and resultant asphyxiation. These crystals can be destroyed by boiling. Despite numerous records of the starchy rootstock being eaten by Native Americans, all of our attempts have met with unmitigated failure. We found it bitter and unpalatable.

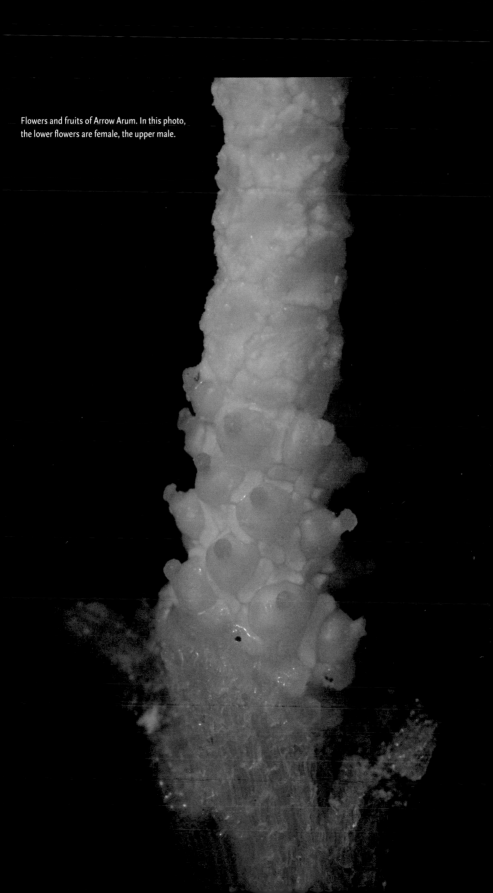

Flowers and fruits of Arrow Arum. In this photo, the lower flowers are female, the upper male.

Arrow-leaf plants in a dense freshwater tidal marsh. Note the widespread sinus between the leaf lobes (*opposite*). The starchy storage organs are formed at the end of the growing season.

Arrowleaf, *Sagittaria latifolia*

Arrowleaf may not be the most appropriate name for *Sagittaria latifolia* because the arrow-leaf motif is found in other marsh plants, several of which are found in the Bay. *Sagittaria latifolia* has another common name, Duck Potato—a reference to the starchy storage organ produced at the end of the growing season, a feature not found in any other arrow-leaf plants.

DISTINGUISHING FEATURES: All plants of this species have arrow-shaped leaves, but the leaf can vary amazingly from extremely narrow arrows to broad, blunt arrowhead leaves. In the narrowest, the lobes of the leaf are only 0.2 in. wide; in the more frequent manifestation, the leaves are up to 2.5 ft. wide. Both extremes are present in the Bay. In addition, all have a milky latex, unlike any other arrow-leaf marsh plant. The vegetative stem is very short and buried in the mud from which the leaves arise. Flowering stalks appear in late spring through fall and are up to 5 ft. tall, bearing large, white flowers. Each flower is unisexual. The fruit, found in the fall, consists of small, flat seeds with a lateral beak that clings to clothing and fur. As winter approaches, the plant produces specialized storage organs at the tip of short, underground stems. These have large amounts of starch and a growing tip. Plants die back to the storage organ in the late fall.

HABITAT: Intolerant of salinity, Arrowleaf is one of the most frequent plants in freshwater tidal marshes. It can grow submersed, but this is uncommon in Bay waters. Arrowleaf is widespread throughout eastern North America.

(Left) The bottom two flowers are female, the top is male. Flowers are about the diameter of a quarter.
(Right) The arrow-leaf shape in four unrelated Bay marsh plants. *From left to right:* Arrowleaf; Halberd-leaved Tearthumb (*Polygonum arifolium*); Arrow Arum (*Peltandra virginica*); Lizard Tail (*Saururus cernuus*).

Arrowleaf (continued)

CONFUSED WITH: There are three species of the genus in Bay waters. Awl-leaf Sagittaria is a diminutive plant. Lance-leaf Sagittaria can grow with Arrowleaf, but the leaves are not arrow-shaped; the flowers, however, are similar. Arrowleaf can be confused with other arrow-leaf-motif plants. Arrowleaf, however, is readily distinguished from the others by the presence of latex, the very broad sinus, and the pattern of venation in which about ten veins of equal size arise from a central point.

WILDLIFE/ECOLOGICAL VALUE: The storage organs are often cached by small mammals.

HUMAN USES: The storage organs were widely used by Native Americans for food. They have a pleasant taste when boiled or roasted. In our opinion, they are the tastiest of the starch sources in Bay waters.

Striking in beauty, the color and form of the flower is a highly specialized reproductive structure with guides for its pollinators and strategically positioned sexual parts that ensure pollen transfer.

Cardinal Flower, *Lobelia cardinalis*

With its large, bright-scarlet flowers, this species steals the show in summer and fall in freshwater Bay marshes. Nothing matches its color, which is prominently displayed on tall, upright stalks.

DISTINGUISHING FEATURES: Cardinal Flower is a short-lived perennial, up to 6.6 ft. tall. It reproduces by shoots from its base. It has long, toothed leaves. Numerous scarlet flowers appear in the summer, with flowering continuing into the fall. The main attractant of the flower is its remarkable color and structure, which renders the lack of appreciable scent understandable. Ruby-throated hummingbirds, which are the chief pollinators, are attracted by the nectar in the tubular lower part of the flower. Flowers produce a many-seeded capsule.

HABITAT: This is a plant of open, sunny areas along freshwater. In the Bay it is frequent in the diurnally flooded freshwater tidal marshes.

WILDLIFE/ECOLOGICAL VALUE: This is an important food plant for humming-birds.

HUMAN USES: Used as an ornamental plant in gardens. Like other members of the genus, Cardinal Flower contains chemicals that are harmful if ingested.

Water Dayflower forms massive populations that overgrow and shade native plants.

Virginia Dayflower at the edge of a tidal swamp forest.

Dayflowers, *Murdannia keisak* & *Commelina virginica*

One of the dayflowers, Water Dayflower (*Murdannia keisak*), an unwelcome invader from East Asia, is altering habitats of native plants by smothering them with its rapidly growing stems. It is also known by the common name Aneilema (*Aneilema keisak*).

DISTINGUISHING FEATURES: Fleshy stems and leaves that are mucilaginous when broken, and small, three-parted attractive pink-purple flowers are features of the weed Water Dayflower. Seldom more than 1.5 ft. tall, it is usually found in large populations with stems spreading on the ground. Thousands of seeds are produced each year. It can also reproduce by rooting from the stem.

HABITAT: Like most weeds, Water Dayflower is well adapted to a variety of habitats, but it has little tolerance for salinity.

CONFUSED WITH: Another member of the same family, the spiderwort family, Virginia Dayflower (*Commelina virginica*), is a native plant of freshwater marshes. While the overall shape of the leaves is similar to that of Water Dayflower, this plant is tall (up to 5 ft.), with sky-blue flowers.

WILDLIFE/ECOLOGICAL VALUE: Waterfowl eat the seeds as a favored food.

HUMAN USES: To humans, this is a noxious weed.

Halberd-leaved Tearthumb, with its large, halberd-shaped leaves,
clambers over marsh vegetation in pursuit of its victims.

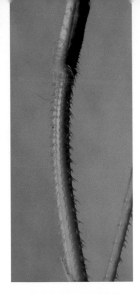

Arrowleaf Tearthumb. The leaves on this species are considerably smaller than those of Halberd-leaved Tearthumb, but if snagged the armament is just as painful.

Halberd-leaved Tearthumb, *Persicaria arifolium*

Tearthumbs tear more than thumbs. Anyone who has traversed freshwater Bay marshes and encountered these plants will know that it is arms and legs that are torn as well. There are two species of these viciously armed plants in the Bay. The not-so-common name of one of them, Halberd-leaved Tearthumb, refers to an instrument of harm—a halberd, a double-headed ax.

DISTINGUISHING FEATURES: Halberd-leaved Tearthumb, an annual, has long stems that climb over vegetation, making formidable thickets by the end of the growing season. Leaves vary considerably in size, but can be up to 1.5 in. long. Flowers are small, various shades of pinkish-white, and produce a single three-sided black seed. It is the armament, however, that makes what literally becomes a lasting impression: the stems are lined with tough, curved prickles that are designed to grab you coming or going—an evolutionary ploy thought to have developed to foster dispersal; for example, a mallard with a necklace of Halberd-leaved Tearthumb might transport seed to the next marsh.

HABITAT: Freshwater to slightly brackish marshes; also along the borders of swamp forests.

CONFUSED WITH: The related Arrowleaf Tearthumb (*Persicaria sagittata*) can be found growing with this species.

WILDLIFE/ECOLOGICAL VALUE: The fruits are an important food for wildlife.

HUMAN USES: There are records of the fruits being eaten.

The attractive flowering heads of Ironweed in a freshwater tidal marsh in midsummer. Wild Rice is evident in the background (*opposite*).

Ironweed, *Vernonia novaboracensis*

Towering over most of its neighbors in a freshwater marsh is Ironweed. Along with blue Pickerel Weed, white Arrowleaf, and the mighty Wild Rice with its distinctive geometry, Ironweed contributes to making a Chesapeake Bay freshwater tidal marsh a place of great beauty in summertime. Graced with masses of purple flowers, Ironweed is readily recognized. The common name is purported to refer to the strength of the stems.

CHARACTERISTICS: A tall (up to 10 ft.), robust perennial with relatively large, toothed leaves arranged in an alternate manner. The stems, crowned with the distinctive purple flowers, late in the season will produce Dandelion-like fruits. The fruits are wind-distributed.

HABITAT: Ironweed is widespread. It is found in a diversity of freshwater wetlands.

CONFUSED WITH: Joe Pye Weeds of the genus *Eupatorium* grow in similar habitats but seldom reach the height of Ironweed.

WILDLIFE/ECOLOGICAL VALUE: None recorded, though butterflies often visit the flowers.

HUMAN USES: Commercially available as a garden plant, Ironweed sometimes exhibits weedy behavior.

(*Left*) Northern Slender Ladies' Tresses.

(*Right*) Nodding Ladies' Tresses in midsummer.

Ladies' Tresses, species of *Spiranthes*

Ladies' Tresses orchids, so-called because of the fancied resemblance of the spiral arrangement of the flowering to ringlets of ladies' hair, are among our commonest orchids. Of the perhaps five species of Ladies' Tresses in the Bay region, we have selected two as examples: Nodding Ladies' Tresses, *Spiranthes cernua*, and the Northern Slender Ladies' Tresses, *Spiranthes lacera* var. *gracilis*.

DISTINGUISHING FEATURES: Nodding Ladies' Tresses grows to about 3 ft. tall. The stem is essentially leafless, the two or three leaves being near the base of the plant. The flowers arise in a graceful spiral; hence, the Latin name *Spiranthes* (spiraled). Each flower is about 1 in. long and creamy white. Like many orchids, the flowers are turned 180 degrees as they develop. The fruit is a capsule with thousands of dust-like seeds.

Northern Slender Ladies' Tresses has the features characteristic of the genus: spirally arranged flowers on an essentially leafless stem. But this orchid is much smaller, about 20 in. high and much narrower. The flowers are likewise—small, seldom more than 0.1 in. long.

HABITAT: Nodding Ladies' Tresses prefers freshwater marshes in open sunny areas. While large stands of these are striking, individual plants are often hidden among other vegetation. Northern Slender Ladies' Tresses prefers somewhat drier habitats and is found at the border of marshes and forests.

A stand of Nodding Ladies' Tresses.

CONFUSED WITH: The other species of the genus, which are distinguished by technical differences, are less frequent in Bay wetlands.

WILDLIFE/ECOLOGICAL VALUE: Unknown.

HUMAN USES: Some varieties have been developed for gardens.

A large population of Lizard Tail in late summer (*opposite*), with developing fruits.

Lizard Tail, *Saururus cernuus*

The colorful common name is directly from the Latin: *saururus* (lizard); *cernuus* (tail). A frequent and often abundant element of freshwater marshes, Lizard Tail is unforgettable.

DISTINGUISHING FEATURES: Like many other marsh occupants, Lizard Tail produces extensive branching underground stems from which the stems with their heart-shaped leaves develop. Leaves are 30 in. long and have a root-beer-like aroma. Stems and leaves die back in the winter. The small, white, fragrant flowers provide an attractive display in midsummer, quickly giving way to the developing seed capsules. One of the distinctive aspects of this species is the way the first flowers are produced at the base of the flowering stalk; as the first flowers open, more develop higher up the stalk, toward the curved, characteristic bent tip. After pollination and as the fruit matures, the stalks straighten.

HABITAT: A common plant of freshwater marshes, Lizard Tail is able to survive in partial shade.

CONFUSED WITH: The leaves of Lizard Tail resemble those of other species with arrow-shaped leaves.

WILDLIFE/ECOLOGICAL VALUE: None recorded.

HUMAN USES: Sometimes planted in water gardens because of its tolerance for inundation.

Marsh Fern reproduces by means
of spores, which are produced on
the underside of some of the leaves
(*opposite*). Like all ferns, it does not
produce flowers.

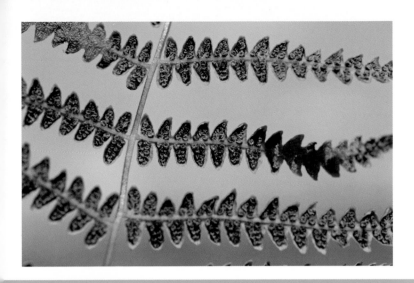

Marsh Fern, *Thelypteris palustris*

The most abundant fern in Bay tidal marshes is the appropriately named Marsh Fern. Often hidden among other vegetation, Marsh Fern is seldom more than 2.5 ft. tall.

DISTINGUISHING FEATURES: Marsh Fern, a perennial, forms large colonies in freshwater marshes, but it is often overlooked when surrounded by larger plants. In spring, it produces the typical "fiddlehead" of most ferns. Spores develop in specialized regions on the underside of the leaf. It dies back in the winter.

HABITAT: Intolerant of saltwater, Marsh Fern is found in the upper reaches of freshwater marshes.

CONFUSED WITH: The New York Fern (*Thelypteris noveboracensis*) resembles the Marsh Fern, but it can be readily determined by the leaf, which is tapered at both ends. In contrast, the bottom part of the Marsh Fern is abruptly truncated. A third species, Massachusetts Fern (*Thelypteris simulata*), infrequent in the Bay, has to be distinguished by technical characteristics.

WILDLIFE/ECOLOGICAL VALUE: There is some evidence that Marsh Fern can be used to mitigate arsenic in soils because of its active uptake of that element.

HUMAN USES: None recorded.

In the fall, the fruiting stalks of Pickerel Weed often bend into the water, where the fruits develop.

(*Opposite*)
Pickerel Weed adds much color to the Bay marshes with its sky-blue flowers spotted with yellow.

Pickerel Weed, *Pontederia cordata*

Pickerel Weed is one of the most common and distinctive of all Chesapeake Bay emergent water plants. The bright-blue flowers and leaves with heart-shaped bases (cordate provides the specific epithet *cordata*), often occurring in large, uniform stands, makes it one of the easiest of all Bay plants to recognize.

DISTINGUISHING FEATURES: This is an emergent, up to 3.5 ft. tall, with leaves arising from the rootstock. The flowering stalk has one leaf. Flowers are usually bright-blue (rarely white) with distinct yellow spots. No other Bay plant has this set of characteristics. Fruits are single-seeded. As they mature, the fruit stalk may be submersed. The seeds germinate underwater.

HABITAT: Entirely freshwater. Pickerel Weed flowers for much of the summer and often forms spectacular displays throughout its range in eastern North America.

CONFUSED WITH: Among other hydrophytes with arrow-shaped leaves and heart-shaped bases are Arrowhead, Arrow Arum, Lizard Tail, and Arrow-leaf Tearthumb.

HUMAN USES: The seeds are reported to be edible, but we have not eaten them.

The large, bright-yellow flowers of Rush-like Bladderwort are striking, even when it is growing among other plants. The bladders in this species are small, barely visible to the naked eye, and have tentacles that attract their prey (*opposite*).

Rush-like Bladderwort, *Utricularia juncea*

In terms of diet, Bladderworts are arguably the most fascinating plants of the Bay: they are carnivorous. They supplement their nutritional intake by capturing and eating small invertebrate animals. The flowers are strikingly beautiful and are sometimes mistaken for orchids. Several species can be found in Bay wetlands; we have chosen one of the most showy as an example.

CHARACTERISTICS: These are small plants, seldom 1 ft. tall, and lack typical leaves. The flower stem is thin and narrow; hence, the use of the word *rush* in the common name. Unlike a rush, it bears large, beautiful flowers in summer. Flowers are up to 3 in. long. A capsule forms later, filled with small seeds. It is the unseen part of the plant, however, that draws so much attention. In the water or mud, myriads of tiny bladders are produced. Water is removed, putting the bladder under negative pressure. Lured by tentacles, small animals trip the mechanism, which causes the door of the trap to open rapidly, sucking in the unsuspecting prey. The animal is digested by secretions within the bladder.

HABITAT: Several species of Bladderwort grow in the Bay region, all of them in freshwater.

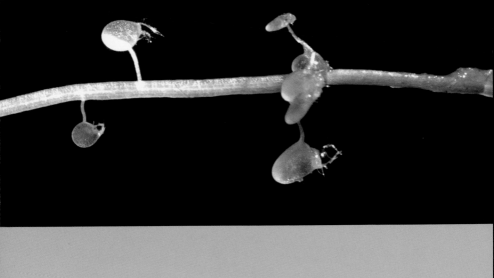

CONFUSED WITH: Nothing. Dwarf Bladderwort, *Utricularia subulata*, can be found in Bay waters and shores. It is a tiny plant, only a few inches tall. Common Bladderwort, *Utricularia vulgaris*, a true aquatic, is found only in water. It has yellow flowers.

WILDLIFE/ECOLOGICAL VALUE: None recorded.

HUMAN USES: Intrinsically interesting for its beautiful flowers and unique mode of nutrition.

(*From left to right*) A large stand of Sensitive-joint Vetch toward the end of its flowering season in September. Stiff hairs cover the entire plant, perhaps as a deterrent to browsing by animals. The butterfly-shaped flowers of Sensitive-joint Vetch are a mark of its affiliation with the bean family.

Sensitive-joint Vetch, *Aeschynomene virginica*

Sensitive-joint Vetch is extremely rare. A federally listed threatened species, Sensitive-joint Vetch maintains some of its largest natural populations in Bay waters. The scientific name translates as "shrinking," but with tall stems rising from the water, this member of the bean family is anything but shrinking in overall size. The name is derived from the species' response to being touched. Some plants are sensitive to touch, folding their leaflets upon contact; hence, the name *Aeschynomene*.

DISTINGUISHING FEATURES: This tall, robust annual grows up to 10 ft. tall. The leaves are compound, with many small leaflets. Like the rest of the plant, leaves are covered with bristly hairs.

The attractive, red-streaked yellow flowers appear in midsummer and give rise to a pod-like structure that breaks into segments.

HABITAT: Fresh to slightly brackish tidal waters, often growing with Wild Rice. Populations can vary in size from year to year.

WILDLIFE/ECOLOGICAL VALUE: None known.

HUMAN USES: The very similar *Aeschynomene indica* has been reported as a weed in rice.

Large population of Smartweed in late summer. This species has white flowers.

A flowering stem (*left*). The flowers are about ¼ in. long. On the right is a stem with the light pink sheath surrounding the stem and the swelling at the base of the leaf.

Smartweed, *Persicaria glabra*

The acrid pungency of the leaves and stems is what gives this plant its common name. Knotweed is another common name because of the swellings on the stem at the base of each leaf.

DISTINGUISHING FEATURES: Stems are up to 3.3 ft. tall, with long, tapering leaves. Conspicuous swellings are present where the leaf leaves the stem. Plants can root from the stems. Flowers are white, producing a flat, black, one-seeded fruit.

HABITAT: Freshwater tidal marshes.

CONFUSED WITH: Similar to False Water-pepper (*Persicaria hydropiperoides*), but that plant has fruits that are triangular in cross section and long hairs on the stems at the base of the leaves.

WILDLIFE/ECOLOGICAL VALUE: The fruits are an important food for wildlife, especially waterfowl.

HUMAN USES: There are records of the fruits being eaten.

The striking posture of Turk's-cap Lily, positioned to maximize availability to pollinators. Dots on the petals guide insects, which must contact the black stamens to obtain nectar. On visiting the next flower, the pollinator deposits pollen on the receptive female part, the black portion at the end of the long tube leading to the ovary.

This Lily is a wetland plant found in marshes or at the margin of a forest and a tidal river. The long flower stems reach out to attract insects.

Turk's-cap Lily, *Lilium superbum*

The widespread and familiar Turk's-cap Lily is an infrequent member of freshwater marshes and river margins in the Bay. Its stunning light orange to reddish flowers are set amid blue Pickerel Weed and scarlet Cardinal Flower in midsummer.

DISTINGUISHING FEATURES: This is one of the largest and most striking of our wildflowers, readily recognized by the brightly colored and curved floral parts. With flowers at the top of long (up to 8 ft.) stems, this lily is designed to provide maximum exposure to the insects that pollinate it. Like other lilies, this species has parts in threes. This symmetry is evident with six leaves arranged in a whorl on the long, strong stem. Also in common with other lilies, Turk's-cap dies back to a bulb at the end of each growing season, leaving the three-part capsule filled with flat seeds.

HABITAT: Freshwater tidal marshes with bulrush, sedges, Arrowleaf, and associated species. It may also be found at the margins of tidal rivers.

WILDLIFE/ECOLOGICAL VALUE: None recorded, though the bulbs are a good source of starch.

HUMAN USES: The starchy bulbs have scales like an onion and were once an emergency food source. But this infrequent marsh beauty should never be dug. It can be easily propagated from seed and makes an attractive garden plant.

Virginia Iris, *Iris virginica*

This is the only plant in the flora of freshwater marshes that sports a large, blue flower. Virginia Iris is the largest of all native irises of the region and often forms large, dense stands.

DISTINGUISHING FEATURES: Like several of its neighbors, Virginia Iris has long leaves (up to 5 ft.), arising from extensive, thick rootstocks. Flowers appear in early spring. These are similar in structure to common garden irises with three-part flowers. Striking in appearance, this is a very pragmatic way for one flower to have three functional pollination units—three flowers for the price of one. The yellow spot directs the pollinating animal, usually a bee, to the nectar. Entering the flower for its reward, the animal is dusted with pollen, which it then carries to the next flower. In the summer the flower yields a three-sided capsule packed with flat seeds.

HABITAT: Freshwater marshes, but it cannot survive constant inundation. Virginia Iris does not tolerate salinity.

A large stand of Virginia Iris in spring. The strap-like leaves can be mistaken for Cattail leaves.

CONFUSED WITH: In its vegetative state, Virginia Iris is easily confused with other strap-shaped marsh plants such as cattails, Sweet Flag, and Bur Reed (see table 3 on p. 147 for a guide to distinguishing them). The introduced European Pale Yellow Iris (*Iris pseudacorus*) has invaded some freshwater marshes of the Bay. It resembles Virginia Iris in its vegetative stage, but is readily distinguished by its pale yellow flowers.

WILDLIFE/ECOLOGICAL VALUE: Seeds are eaten by waterfowl.

HUMAN USES: Planted in water gardens. Some people develop dermatitis from handling the rhizomes, perhaps from the abundant, needle-like crystals characteristic of the genus.

Water Willow, *Justicia americana*

Its aquatic habitat and leaf shape may explain why this is called Water Willow. However, Water Willow, unlike true willows (species of the genus *Salix*), is an herbaceous plant that dies back in the winter.

DISTINGUISHING FEATURES: A long-lived perennial from an extensive, creeping rootstock, Water Willow has leaves arranged alternately; these are elongate and drooping and reminiscent of leaves of true willows. The leafy stems are usually taller than the flowering stems, but the flowers are relatively large and showy. In the Bay region, the flowers are light blue and purple and appear in early to late summer. From these develop a capsule with four seeds. Water Willow is unusual among Bay plants in forcibly ejecting its seeds from the capsule, ensuring that they land in the water or on a site where they can be established.

HABITAT: An obligate aquatic plant, this species is found through much of eastern North America.

Water Willow often grows in dense, uniform stands.

CONFUSED WITH: A related species, Loose-flower Water Willow (*Justicia ovata*), occurs in swamp forests at the extreme southern end of the Bay. However, it is much smaller, does not form dense clumps, and does not grow in standing water.

WILDLIFE/ECOLOGICAL VALUE: Because it grows in water that can be either flowing or still, this species is a nursery for small fish and other animals. The tough rootstock aids in shore and bank stabilization.

HUMAN USES: Sometimes planted in water gardens.

Buttonbush in flower in midsummer. The masses of small fragrant flowers of this coffee relative stand out in freshwater marshes.

SHRUBS

Buttonbush, *Cephalanthus occidentalis*

The appropriately named Buttonbush, an allusion to the spherical fruits, is common in marshes and along streams.

DISTINGUISHING FEATURES: The leaves are up to 6 in. long, glossy, and arranged in an opposite manner on the woody stems. Flowers are borne in globe-like masses in midsummer and attract a diversity of insects, apparently for the nectar. Shrubs can be up to 12 ft. tall and lose their leaves in the fall. In early fall the single-seeded fruits are produced.

HABITAT: Common in freshwater marshes, along streams, and at margins of swamps.

WILDLIFE/ECOLOGICAL VALUE: Seeds are eaten by waterfowl.

HUMAN USES: Sometimes planted for its ornamental value and as a butterfly plant.

(*Opposite*) Developing Buttonbrush fruits in late summer.

Poison Sumac showing the diagnostic features of the leaves with
9 to 11 leaflets and a red leaf stalk. This specimen is flowering.

Poison Sumac, *Toxicodendron vernix*

This shrub or small tree is infrequently seen in Bay wetlands, but it takes only one inadvertent encounter by someone who is susceptible for it to become memorable. The reaction is the same as that caused by Poison Ivy, but because Poison Sumac is larger more contact is possible. Also frequently known as *Rhus vernix*.

DISTINGUISHING FEATURES: One of the insidious features of this dangerous shrub (it can be a small tree in other parts of its range) is how ordinary it looks: just a harmless, nondescript shrub at the edge of a wetland. Usually plants are less than 10 ft. tall, with large leaves, 3 ft. long and composed of an odd number of leaflets. These leaflets are arranged opposite one another on the characteristically red leaf stalk, with a single leaflet at the tip. In older shrubs, the bark is grey. Flowers are produced in early summer, and, in character with the plant, these are also green and nondescript. The white, berry-like fruits appear in the fall and sometimes persist through the winter.

HABITAT: In northern bogs, Poison Sumac can produce a dense, uniform stand of dangerous trunks. In the Bay region, plants are usually solitary and prefer the margins between wetlands and uplands.

CONFUSED WITH: This is one of a group of shrubs called Sumacs—woody plants, shrubs, or small trees with large leaves arranged in an alternate manner. Several widespread Sumacs, all in the genus *Rhus*, have leaves similar to those of Poison Sumac, but none of the other Sumacs cause dermatitis. Some have edible fruits.

Readily distinguished from Poison Sumac by their red, hairy fruits and leaf segments with teeth, they do not occur in wetlands.

WILDLIFE/ECOLOGICAL VALUE: Notwithstanding the danger it poses to humans, some birds eat the fruits and numerous insects visit the dull flowers.

HUMAN USES: Warning! This is a dangerous plant that can cause great suffering. All parts of the plants are considered to be dermatitis-causing in all seasons.

Seaside Alder, *Alnus maritima*

The genus name *Alnus* is simply the ancient Latin name for alder. *Maritima* refers to the coastal tidal habitat where this rare species was first described. It is sometimes known by the common name Delmarva Alder because of the significant populations in that region.

DISTINGUISHING FEATURES: A much-branched, deciduous small tree or large shrub (up to 20 ft.), it is found in slightly brackish to freshwater tidal habitats in the Delmarva Peninsula of Delaware and Maryland. Leaves are not lobed, broadest above the middle, and have a finely toothed margin. The bark is smooth and gray. The persistent woody remains of the fruit resemble a miniature pine cone.

HABITAT: This alder forms dense, localized stands on freshwater tidal rivers in full sun or partial shade along the boundary between freshwater tidal marshes and tidal forested wetlands. Seaside Alder has been reported only from a small number of sites in four states: Delaware, northwest Georgia, Maryland, and southwest Oklahoma; the Chesapeake Bay watershed is one of the last strongholds for this rare species.

CONFUSED WITH: Seaside Alder can grow with another alder species, Brookside Alder (*Alnus serrulata*). Seaside Alder flowers in the autumn, whereas all other North American alders flower in the early spring. Although sometimes found in large populations, Seaside Alder is rare in Bay waters; Brookside Alder, on the other

(Opposite) Flowering Seaside Alder in mid-September, displaying male flowers. The same shrub produces female flowers that are much smaller.
(Below) Comparison of Alder leaves. *From left to right:* Seaside Alder upper surface, Brookside Alder lower surface, Seaside Alder lower surface, Brookside Alder upper surface.

hand, is very common—a smooth-barked shrub of riparian areas and within freshwater tidal and nontidal wetlands throughout the Chesapeake Bay watershed.

WILDLIFE/ECOLOGICAL VALUE: Alders are important components of wetlands because of their ability to use atmospheric nitrogen and convert it into a usable form. This is often reflected in the darker-green color of alder compared with leaves of neighboring plants.

HUMAN USES: Few reported, although alders in general have been used as a folk remedy for a variety of ailments (e.g., as a cure for digestive problems, a remedy for burns and bruises, and as an antimalarial medicine). The inner bark of various alders has been used as an emergency food. Seaside Alder is reported to be easily propagated from seed. It may have limited value as an ornamental.

The Swamp Rose has 5 petals and leaves with 5 to 7 leaflets.

Fruits of Swamp Rose.

Swamp Rose, *Rosa palustris*

Swamp Rose is the most common native rose in the region. It is a common component of freshwater wetlands, including the Bay.

DISTINGUISHING FEATURES: A much-branched deciduous shrub, Swamp Rose grows to 10 ft. tall and has alternately arranged leaves that, in turn, are divided into five leaflets. One of the earliest Bay marsh shrubs to flower, the large flowers, 3 in. in diameter, have attractive pink petals. From the fragrant flowers arise the typical fruits that in roses are known as hips. Swamp Rose hips are covered with stiff, prickly hairs.

HABITAT: Freshwater marshes. Swamp Rose has some tolerance for salinity. Widespread in eastern North America.

CONFUSED WITH: No other armed shrubs appear in freshwater marshes of the Bay.

WILDLIFE/ECOLOGICAL VALUE: The armed branches provide nesting sites for birds. Fruits are eaten by wildlife.

HUMAN USES: The fruits are edible and high in vitamin C. However, the seeds have stiff hairs that can irritate the digestive system. Sometimes planted in water gardens.

A young, vigorous branch of Poison Ivy among Salt Grass in a salt marsh.

Poison Ivy in autumn with characteristic crimson coloration. The white, berry-like fruits are evident.

Poison Ivy, *Toxicodendron radicans*

Poison Ivy grows anywhere and everywhere. It is one of the most common woody vines in Bay wetlands, occasionally being found even at the margins of salt marshes.

DISTINGUISHING FEATURES. Warning! All parts of the plant are toxic at all seasons. Poison Ivy has alternate leaves that are divided into three parts. The terminal part, or leaflet, is symmetrical; that is, both sides of the mid-rib are the same. On the other hand, the two lower leaflets are asymmetrical. As if to give warning of its venom, Poison Ivy often displays spectacular crimson fall color before the leaves fall.

Flowers are green, inconspicuous, and appear in the spring. Ghostly grey-white fruits are mature in the late summer and fall. Poison Ivy is a woody vine, attaching itself to its substrate by small, specialized reddish roots that give large vines a hairy appearance.

HABITAT: Anywhere.

CONFUSED WITH: Just about any climbing woody vine, especially Virginia Creeper (*Parthenocissus quinquefolia*), which often grows with Poison Ivy, sometimes intertwined on the same tree. Virginia creeper, however, has five leaflets and blue-black fruits. A simple reminder of how to distinguish them is the old saying, "Leaves of three, let it be. Leaves of five, stay alive."

WILDLIFE/ECOLOGICAL VALUE: Inexplicably, birds eat the fruits of Poison Ivy.

HUMAN USES: Thousands of people every year learn about this plant through the pain it inflicts on them.

(*Left*) Bald Cypress in its autumnal foliage with mature cones. (*Right*) Summer foliage.

Bald Cypress, *Taxodium distichum*

Bald Cypress is said to be bald because it drops its leaf in the winter, an unusual feature for a gymnosperm. It is one of the best-known and best-loved trees of swamp forests in the southeastern United States. Not a true cypress, it likely received the name from pioneers who equated it with Cypress (*Cupressus sempervirens*), a widely distributed Mediterranean tree mentioned in the Bible. It seldom grows north of the Bay.

DISTINGUISHING FEATURES: A large tree with bark peeling in narrow strips on mature trees, Bald Cypress is unusual in being a gymnosperm that lives in aquatic situations. In fact, it is one of only a few trees that can thrive in standing water. The bases of the trees are buttressed, or swollen, a feature typically found among Bay trees only in Bald Cypress, Tupelo, and Pumpkin Ash. Leaves are small, needle-like, and about 0.3 in. long. The leaves turn brown in the fall. While it is often referred to as having deciduous leaves, it is actually the short branches that fall. Reproductive structures are unisexual, although each tree bears both sexes. Male cones are tiny and borne in chains that dangle in the air to release pollen to the tiny, inconspicuous female structures. The latter then develop cones. The cones are globe-shaped and green when mature. They open to release small seeds, which are airborne. What readily distinguishes this tree from any other in the flora is the production of specialized roots, commonly known as knees because of their shape. The function of these has been debated. They could be organs that allow air to enter the roots, essential for a plant living in standing water, or, they could be instruments of stabilization, also essential in an aquatic habitat.

A large Bald Cypress in a freshwater tidal marsh. Note the extensive knees.

HABITAT: Moist soil or standing water. While Bald Cypress is adapted to life in water, the seeds will germinate and establish seedlings only on dry or moist soil. This tree has little tolerance for salinity.

WILDLIFE/ECOLOGICAL VALUE: Important as a site for birds and small mammals, Bald Cypress is a keystone species in swamp systems, including freshwater tidal swamps, in Bay waters.

HUMAN USES: Long valued for its decay-resistant timber, Bald Cypress is still used in the production of caskets and shingles.

(*Left*) Leaves and fruits of Pumpkin Ash in September. The leaf stalks are longer than in other Ashes.

(*Right*) Leaflets of three wetland Ashes. The middle is Pumpkin Ash, with Green Ash on the left and Carolina Ash on the right.

Pumpkin Ash, *Fraxinus profunda*

Three species of ash trees are found in Bay wetlands: Water Ash (*Fraxinus caroliniana*), Green Ash (*Fraxinus pennsylvanica*), and Pumpkin Ash (*Fraxinus profunda*). Pumpkin Ash is so named because the base of the tree is often buttressed, giving a fanciful resemblance to a pumpkin. This shape is also reflected in the name Butt Ash.

DISTINGUISHING FEATURES: Like all ashes, leaves are opposite and compound, with 5 to 7 leaflets, one of which is terminal. Each of the leaflets is 5 in. long, on a short leaf stalk that is densely hairy, especially on young leaves.

Pumpkin Ash, like all its congeners, is unisexual; that is, each tree is either male or female. Flowers are green, inconspicuous, and apparently pollinated by wind. The flowers appear before the leaves. Fruits are one-seeded, long, and narrow, with a wing that aids in wind dispersal.

HABITAT: Pumpkin Ash is one of the few trees that can grow in standing water. Like the other arboreal water denizens—Bald Cypress and Tupelo—it develops a buttressed base.

Fruits of the three wetland Ashes of the Bay. *From left to right:* Pumpkin Ash, Water Ash, Green Ash. Fruits of all three species are produced about the same time in autumn.

CONFUSED WITH: Other Ashes—Water Ash and Green Ash. Like Pumpkin Ash, Water Ash can also be found in tidal freshwater hardwood swamps. Green Ash favors less saturated sites than the other two. Pumpkin Ash is hairier than the other two and has the narrowest wings on its fruits.

WILDLIFE/ECOLOGICAL VALUE: The fruits are eaten by birds.

HUMAN USES: The wood of Pumpkin Ash is valued for tool handles and other applications where a hard, durable wood is needed.

Red Maple begins and ends the year with red. These leaves are just ready to fall (*opposite, top*). In early spring, red flowers are produced (*right*); they arise from red buds, seen below the flower, on red twigs. These flowers produce red fruits within a few weeks of opening.

Red Maple, *Acer rubrum*

This tree is one of the most abundant in the region. It is aptly named red since that color can be found on some part of the tree in each season of the year.

DISTINGUISHING FEATURES: Unlike many forest trees, Red Maple often has several trunks arising from the base of the tree. The bark is ashen grey and quite variable in its pattern. Like all maples, the leaves are arranged in an opposite manner. Maples and ashes are the only trees in the Bay area that have this arrangement. The sex life of Red Maple is more confusing than a soap opera: trees can have flowers that are mainly bisexual, mainly unisexual, or any combination of those. Sexual reproduction is obviously successful, however, since hundreds of thousands of airborne fruits shower down in the spring.

HABITAT: Red Maple is opportunistic and can grow in a variety of habitats. But it is able to survive in saturated soils and therefore forms an important component of Bay swamps.

CONFUSED WITH: Silver Maple (*Acer saccharinum*) is native, but much less common than Red Maple. It, too, grows in swamps, but it is seldom encountered in the Bay. Another common tree, Sweet Gum (*Liquidambar styraciflua*), is sometimes confused with maples. However, the leaves of Sweet Gum are borne alternately and have an overall star shape, with all lobes of approximately equal size. The fruit is the familiar gum ball.

Silver Maple leaves have lobes that are at least twice as long as wide, and each lobe is deeply toothed. The name Silver Maple comes from the color of the leaf undersurface. This tree does not have the conspicuous red coloring of its showy relative maple.

WILDLIFE/ECOLOGICAL VALUE: Because the wood decays readily, Red Maple provides excellent nesting sites for birds and small mammals. The buds are eaten by squirrels during the winter.

HUMAN USES: The wood of Red Maple is considered of low quality; it is, however, sometimes used in furniture. The seeds are edible, but scarcely palatable.

Fruits and a seed of Tupelo. The fruits are the size of a small olive.

Tupelo, *Nyssa aquatica*

There is an enduring charm about this denizen of freshwater tidal swamps, its bulbous base rising out of standing water. It is restricted to the southern portions of the Bay. It is frequently known as Water Tupelo.

DISTINGUISHING FEATURES: Often growing to a very large size, Tupelo has large, thin leaves, about 1.5 ft. long in an alternate pattern. These characteristically turn a bright yellow before falling. Flowers are produced early in the spring, about the time the leaves appear. Yellow-green in color, they are favored by bees, producing a highly valued honey. Most Tupelo are unisexual, and fruits are produced only on the female trees. The fruits, which resemble small black olives, are water-dispersed. The seed is enclosed in a spongy tissue that allows the fruits to float, making them readily collectable by wildlife.

HABITAT: Moist soil or standing water. Like its frequent companion, Bald Cypress, Tupelo is adapted to life in water. The seeds will germinate and establish seedlings only on dry or moist soil.

CONFUSED WITH: Tupelo shares several adaptations to its swamp environment with Bald Cypress and this has given a similar appearance to both. Tupelo, however, is readily distinguished by its large leaves and distinctive fruit.

WILDLIFE/ECOLOGICAL VALUE: Important to a variety of wildlife for food and habitat.

A Tupelo stand in late summer showing the diagnostic buttressed bases, large leaves, and developing fruit.

HUMAN USES: Because Tupelo usually has a long bole (the distance from the ground to the first branch) it is a valuable timber tree, used for furniture and in construction projects.

Appendix

Scientific Names, Authors, and
Families of Plants of the Chesapeake Bay

COMMON NAME	COMMON NAME SYNONYM	SCIENTIFIC NAME	SCIENTIFIC NAME SYNONYM	FAMILY
American Lotus	Yellow Lotus	*Nelumbo lutea* Willd.	*Nelumbo nucifera* ssp. *lutea* Borsch. & Barthlott	Nelumbonaceae
Arrow Arum	Green Arrow Arum	*Peltandra virginica* (L.) Schott		Araceae
Arrowleaf	Broadleaf Arrowhead	*Sagittaria latifolia* Willd.	*Sagittaria variabilis* Engelm. ex A. Gray var. *latifolia* (Willd.) Engelm.; *Sagittaria sagittifolia* L. f. *latifolia* (Willd.) Britton	Alismataceae
Bald Cypress		*Taxodium distichum* (L.) Rich.		Cupressaceae (Taxodiaceae)
Beach Grass	American Beachgrass	*Ammophila breviligulata* Fernald		Poaceae
Beach Panic Grass	Bitter Panicgrass	*Panicum amarum* Elliott	*Chasea amara* (Elliott) Nieuwl.	Poaceae
Beach Spurge	Small Seaside Sandmat	*Euphorbia polygonifolia* L.	*Chamaesyce polygonifolia* (L.) Small	Euphorbiaceae
Beach Vitex	Round-leaf Chastetree	*Vitex rotundifolia* L. f.		Lamiaceae (Verbenaceae)
Big Cord Grass		*Spartina cynosuroides* (L.) Roth	*Dactylis cynosuroides* L.	Poaceae
Bladderwort	Southern Bladderwort	*Utricularia juncea* Vahl	*Stomoisia juncea* Barnhart	Lentibulariaceae

COMMON NAME	COMMON NAME SYNONYM	SCIENTIFIC NAME	SCIENTIFIC NAME SYNONYM	FAMILY
Bottle-brush Sedge	Longhair Sedge	*Carex comosa* Boott	*Carex pseudo-cyperus* L. var. *comosa* (Boott) Boott	Cyperaceae
Broad-leaf Cattail		*Typha latifolia* L.		Typhaceae
Bur Reed	American Bur-reed	*Sparganium americanum* Nutt.	*Sparganium simplex* Huds. var. *americanum* Farw.	Sparganiaceae (Typhaceae)
Buttonbush		*Cephalanthus occidentalis* L.		Rubiaceae
Cardinal Flower		*Lobelia cardinalis* L.	*Dortmanna cardinalis* (L.) Kuntze; *Rapuntium cardinale* (L.) Mill.	Campanulaceae
Coast Cockspur Grass		*Echinochloa walteri* (Pursh) A. Heller	*Panicum walteri* Pursh	Poaceae
Collared Dodder	Bigseed Alfalfa Dodder	*Cuscuta indecora* Choisy	*Cuscuta decora* var. *indecora* (Choisy) Engelm.; *Grammica indecora* (Choisy) W. A. Weber; *Epithymum indecorum* (Choisy) Nieuwl. & Lunell	Cuscutaceae (Convolvulaceae)
Creeping Rush	Lesser Creeping Rush	*Juncus repens* Michx.		Juncaceae
Cypress Swamp Sedge		*Carex joorii* L. H. Bailey		Cyperaceae
Dandelion		*Taraxacum officinale* F. H. Wigg.	*Leontodon officinale* L.	Asteraceae
Dwarf Glasswort	Dwarf Saltwort	*Salicornia bigelovii* Torr.		Amaranthaceae (Chenopodiaceae)

COMMON NAME	COMMON NAME SYNONYM	SCIENTIFIC NAME	SCIENTIFIC NAME SYNONYM	FAMILY
Dwarf Sagittaria	Awl-leaf Arrowhead	*Sagittaria subulata* (L.) Buchenau		Alismataceae
Eel Grass	Seawrack	*Zostera marina* L.		Zosteraceae
Evergreen Quillwort		*Isoetes hyemalis* D. F. Brunton		Isoetaceae
Fox Sedge		*Carex vulpi-noidea* Michx.		Cyperaceae
Fringed Sedge		*Carex crinita* Lam.		Cyperaceae
Giant Sedge		*Carex gigantea* Rudge	*Carex lacustris* var. *gigantea* (Rudge) Pursh; *Carex lupulina* Muhl. ex Willd. var. *gigantea* Britton; *Carex grandis* L. H. Bailey	Cyperaceae
Grasswort	Eastern Grasswort	*Lilaeopsis chinensis* (L.) Kuntze	*Hydrocotyle chinensis* L.	Apiaceae
Groundsel Tree	Eastern Baccharis	*Baccharis halimi-folia* L.		Asteraceae
Hackberry	Sugarberry	*Celtis laevigata* Willd.	*Mertensia laevi-gata* Kunth.	Ulmaceae (Cannabaceae)
Hair-like Spikerush	Needle Spikerush	*Eleocharis acicu-laris* (L.) Roem. & Schult.	*Scirpus acicularis* L.	Cyperaceae
Hercules' Club	Toothache Tree	*Zanthoxylum clava-herculis* L.	*Zanthoxylum ayua* M. Gomez; *Fagara clava-herculis* Small	Rutaceae
Hornwort	Coon's Tail	*Ceratophyllum demersum* L.		Ceratophyll-aceae
Hydrilla	Waterthyme	*Hydrilla verticil-lata* (L.f.) Royle	*Serpicula verticil-lata* Roxb.	Hydrocharit-aceae
Ironweed	New York Ironweed	*Vernonia nove-boracensis* (L.) Michx.		Asteraceae

COMMON NAME	COMMON NAME SYNONYM	SCIENTIFIC NAME	SCIENTIFIC NAME SYNONYM	FAMILY
Japanese Sedge		*Carex kobomugi* Ohwi		Cyperaceae
Live Oak		*Quercus virginiana* Mill.		Fagaceae
Lizard Tail		*Saururus cernuus* L.		Saururaceae
Looseflower Water Willow		*Justicia ovata* (Walter) Lindau	*Rhytiglossa ovata* Nees; *Dianthera ovata* Walter	Acanthaceae
Marsh Elder	Jesuit's Bark	*Iva frutescens* L.		Asteraceae
Marsh Fern	Eastern Marsh Fern	*Thelypteris palustris* Schott		Thelypteridaceae
Marsh Fleabane	Sweetscent	*Pluchea odorata* (L.) Cass.		Asteraceae
Mattaponi Quillwort		*Isoetes mattaponica* L. J. Musselman		Isoetaceae
Narrow-leaf Cattail		*Typha angustifolia* L.		Typhaceae
Needle Rush	Needle-grass Rush	*Juncus roemarianus* Scheele		Juncaceae
Nodding Ladies' Tresses		*Spiranthes cernua* (L.) Rich.	*Ophrys cernua* L.	Orchidaceae
Northern Slender Ladies' Tresses		*Spiranthes lacera* (Raf.) Raf. var. *gracilis* (Bigelow) Luer	*Neottia gracilis* Bigelow	Orchidaceae
Orache	Spear Saltbush	*Atriplex patula* L.	*Atriplex hastata* var. *patula* Farw.; *Atriplex patula* ssp. *typica* H. M. Hall & Clem.	Amaranthaceae (Chenopodiaceae)
Perennial Glasswort	Virginia Glasswort	*Sarcocornia pacifica* (Standley) A. J. Scott	*Salicornia virginica* L.	Amaranthaceae (Chenopodiaceae)
Pickerel Weed		*Pontederia cordata* L.	*Unisema cordata* (L.) Farw.; *Narukila cordata* (L.) Nieuwl.	Pontederiaceae

COMMON NAME	COMMON NAME SYNONYM	SCIENTIFIC NAME	SCIENTIFIC NAME SYNONYM	FAMILY
Pipewort	Estuary Pipewort	*Eriocaulon parkeri* B. L. Rob.	*Eriocaulon septangulare* With. var. *parkeri* (B. L. Rob.) B. Boivin & Cay.	Eriocaulaceae
Poison Ivy	Eastern Poison Ivy	*Toxicodendron radicans* (L.) Kuntze	*Rhus radicans* L.	Anacardiaceae
Poison Sumac		*Toxicodendron vernix* (L.) Kuntze	*Rhus vernix* L.	Anacardiaceae
Pumpkin Ash		*Fraxinus profunda* (Bush) Bush	*Fraxinus pennsylvanica* var. *profunda* Lingelsh.; *Calycomelia profunda* Nieuwl.; *Fraxinus americana* var. *profunda* Bush	Oleaceae
Red Maple		*Acer rubrum* L.	*Rufacer rubrum* (L.) Small	Sapindaceae (Aceraceae)
Salt Grass		*Distichlis spicata* (L.) Greene	*Uniola spicata* L.	Poaceae
Salt-marsh Aster	Perennial Salt-marsh Aster	*Aster tenuifolium* L.	*Symphyotrichum tenuifolium* (L.) G. L. Nesom	Asteraceae
Salt-marsh Bulrush	Study Bulrush	*Bolboschoenus robustus* (Pursh) Soják	*Schoenoplectus robustus* (Pursh) M. T. Strong; *Scirpus maritimus* L. var. *macrostachyus* Michx.; *Scirpus robustus* Pursh	Cyperaceae

COMMON NAME	COMMON NAME SYNONYM	SCIENTIFIC NAME	SCIENTIFIC NAME SYNONYM	FAMILY
Salt-marsh Cord Grass	Smooth Cord Grass	*Spartina alterniflora* Loisel	*Spartina stricta* var. *alterniflora* (Loisel) A. Gray; *Spartina glabra* Muhl. var. *alterniflora* (Loisel) Merr.; *Spartina maritima* Fernald var. *alterniflora* (Loisel) St. Yves	Poaceae
Salt-meadow Cord Grass		*Spartina patens* (Aiton) Muhl.	*Dactylis patens* Aiton	Poaceae
Samphire		*Salicornia virginica* L.	*Salicornia europaea* L.; *Salicornia maritima* Wolff & Jefferies	Amaranthaceae (Chenopodiaceae)
Sandspur	Mat Sandbur	*Cenchrus longispinus* (Hack.) Fernald	*Cenchrus echinatus* L. f. *longispinus* Hack.	Poaceae
Sea Lavender	Lavender Thrift	*Limonium carolinianum* (Walter) Britton	*Statice carolinianum* Walter; *Statice limonium* Bigelow var. *carolinianum* A. Gray	Plumbaginaceae
Sea Oats		*Uniola paniculata* L.	*Uniola maritima* Michx.; *Nevroctola maritima* Raf. ex B. D. Jacks.	Poaceae
Sea Oxeye	Bushy Seaside Tansy	*Borrichia frutescens* (L.) DC.	*Buphthalmum frutescens* L.	Asteraceae
Sea Rocket	American Sea Rocket	*Cakile edentula* (Bigelow) Hook.		Brassicaceae
Seashore Mallow	Virginia Salt-marsh Mallow	*Kosteletzkya virginica* (L.) C. Presl ex A. Gray	*Hibiscus virginica* L.	Malvaceae
Seaside Alder		*Alnus maritima* (Marsh.) Muhl. ex Nutt.		Betulaceae

COMMON NAME	COMMON NAME SYNONYM	SCIENTIFIC NAME	SCIENTIFIC NAME SYNONYM	FAMILY
Seaside Gerardia	Salt-marsh False Foxglove	*Agalinis maritima* (Raf.) Raf.		Orobanchaceae (Scrophulariaceae)
Seaside Goldenrod		*Solidago sempervirens* L.	*Aster sempervirens* Kuntze	Asteraceae
Sensitive-joint Vetch	Virginia Joint-vetch	*Aeschynomene virginica* (L.) Britton, Sterns, & Poggenb.	*Hedysarum virginicum* L.	Fabaceae
Short-bristled Horned-beak Sedge		*Rhynchospora corniculata* (Lam.) A. Gray	*Schoenus corniculatus* Lam.	Cyperaceae
Slender Marsh Pink	Slender Rose Gentian	*Sabatia campanulata* (L.) Torr.	*Sabatia gracilis* Salisb.	Gentianaceae
Small Spike Rush	Dwarf Spikerush	*Eleocharis parvula* (Roem. & Schult.) Link ex Bluff, Nees, & Schauer	*Scirpus parvulus* Roem. & Schult.	Cyperaceae
Smartweed	Denseflower Knotweed	*Persicaria glabra* (Willd.) M. Gomez	*Polygonum glabrum* Willd.	Polygonaceae
Soft-stem Bulrush		*Schoenoplectus tabernaemontani* (C. C. Gmel.) Palla		Cyperaceae
Soft-stem Rush	Common Rush	*Juncus effusus* L.		Juncaceae
Southern Sea Blite	Annual Seepweed	*Suaeda linearis* (Elliott) Moq.	*Salsola linearis* Elliott	Amaranthaceae (Chenopodiaceae)
Southern Water Nymph		*Najas guadalupensis* (Spreng.) Magnus	*Najas microdon* Morong; *Caulinia guadalupensis* Spreng.	Najadaceae (Hydrocharitaceae)
Southern Wild Rice	Giant Cutgrass	*Zizaniopsis miliacea* (Michx.) Döll & Asch.	*Zizania miliacea* Michx.	Poaceae

COMMON NAME	COMMON NAME SYNONYM	SCIENTIFIC NAME	SCIENTIFIC NAME SYNONYM	FAMILY
Square-stem Spikerush		*Eleocharis quadrangulata* (Michx.) Roem. & Schult.		Cyperaceae
Swamp Dodder	Scaldweed	*Cuscuta gronovii* Willd. ex Schult.	*Epithymum gronovii* (Roem. & Shult.) Nieuwl. & Lunell; *Grammica gronovii* (Roem. & Schult.) Hadac & Chrtek	Cuscutaceae (Convolvulaceae)
Swamp Rose		*Rosa palustris* Marsh.		Rosaceae
Sweet Flag	Calamus	*Acorus calamus* L.		Acoraceae
Tall Horned-beak Sedge		*Rhynchospora macrostachya* Torr. ex A. Gray	*Rhynchospora corniculata* var. *macrostachya* (Torr. ex A. Gray) Britton	Cyperaceae
Tearthumb	Halberd-leaved Tearthumb	*Persicaria arifolium* (L.) Haralds. *Polygonum arifolium* L.	*Polygonum arifolium* L. *Truellum arifolium* (L.) Soják; *Tracaulon arifolium* (L.) Raf.	Polygonaceae
Three-square Bulrush	Chairmaker's Bulrush	*Schoenoplectus americanus* (Pers.) Volkart ex Schinz & R. Keller	*Scirpus americanus* Pers.	Cyperaceae
Tupelo	Water Tupelo	*Nyssa aquatica* L.		Cornaceae
Turk's-cap Lily		*Lilium superbum* L.	*Lilium canadense* ssp. *superbum* (L.) Baker	Liliaceae
Virginia Iris		*Iris virginica* L.	*Iris versicolor* var. *virginica* (L.) Baker	Iridaceae

COMMON NAME	COMMON NAME SYNONYM	SCIENTIFIC NAME	SCIENTIFIC NAME SYNONYM	FAMILY
Water Dayflower	Wart Removing Herb	*Murdannia keisak* (Hassk.) Hand.-Maz.	*Aneilema keisak* Hasskarl	Commelinaceae
Water Flaxseed	Dotted Duckmeat	*Spirodela oligorrhiza* (Kurz) Hegelm.	*Landoltia punctata* (G. Mey.) D. H. Les & D. J. Crawford; *Lemna oligorrhiza* Kurz; *Spirodela punctata* (G. Mey.) C. H. Thomp.	Lemnaceae
Water Willow	American Water Willow	*Justicia americana* (L.) Vahl.	*Dianthera americana* L.	Acanthaceae
Waterwort	American Waterwort	*Elatine americana* (Pursh) Arn.	*Potamopitys americana* Kuntze	Elatinaceae
White Loosestrife	Wand Lythrum	*Lythrum lineare* L.		Lythraceae
White Water Lily	American White Water Lily	*Nymphaea odorata* Aiton	*Leuconymphaea odorata* MacMill.; *Castalia odorata* (Aiton) Wood	Nymphaeaceae
Wigeon Grass	Widgeon Grass	*Ruppia maritima* L.	*Buccaferrea maritima* Lunell	Potamogetonaceae (Ruppiaceae)
Wild Rice	Annual Wild Rice	*Zizania aquatica* L.	*Ceratochaete aquatica* (L.) Lunell	Poaceae
Yellow Water Lily	Yellow Pond Lily	*Nuphar lutea* (L.) Sm.		Nymphaeaceae

Index of Scientific Names

Page numbers in bold indicate species descriptions.

General Index

Lists common names of plants not included in the Contents

The Johns Hopkins University Press
2715 North Charles Street
Baltimore, Maryland 21218-4363
www.press.jhu.edu

Library of Congress Cataloging-in-Publication Data
Musselman, Lytton J.
Plants of the Chesapeake Bay : a guide to wildflowers, grasses, aquatic vegetation,
trees, shrubs, and other flora / Lytton John Musselman and David A. Knepper.
p. cm.
Includes indexes.
ISBN-13: 978-1-4214-0497-4 (hdbk. : alk. paper)
ISBN-13: 978-1-4214-0498-1 (pbk. : alk. paper)
ISBN-10: 1-4214-0497-4 (hdbk. : alk. paper)
ISBN-10: 1-4214-0498-2 (pbk. : alk. paper)
1. Plants—Chesapeake Bay (Md. and Va.)
I. Knepper, David A., 1963– II. Title.
QK122.8.M87 2012
571.209163'47—dc23   2011026545

A catalog record for this book is available from the British Library.

*Special discounts are available for bulk purchases of this book. For more informa-
tion, please contact Special Sales at 410-516-6936 or specialsales@press.jhu.edu.*

The Johns Hopkins University Press uses environmentally friendly book materials, including
recycled text paper that is composed of at least 30 percent post-consumer waste, whenever possible.